LIFE IS
SETTING ME UP
FOR SUCCESS

VICTOR LEVY

BALBOA.PRESS
A DIVISION OF HAY HOUSE

Balboa Press books may be ordered through booksellers or by contacting:

Balboa Press
A Division of Hay House
1663 Liberty Drive
Bloomington, IN 47403
www.balboapress.com
844-682-1282

Edited by Caroline Guerin

Scripture quotations marked NIV are taken from the Holy Bible, New International Version®. NIV®. Copyright © 1973, 1978, 1984 by International Bible Society. Used by permission of Zondervan. All rights reserved. [Biblica]

Print information available on the last page.

ISBN: 978-1-9822-7643-0 (sc)
ISBN: 978-1-9822-7645-4 (hc)
ISBN: 978-1-9822-7644-7 (e)

Library of Congress Control Number: 2021922205

Balboa Press rev. date: 01/31/2022

Dedicated to my mom

CONTENTS

I HOPE YOU NEVER ACCOMPLISH YOUR GOALS

MOST PEOPLE LIVE LIFE AS IF IT IS A RACE. EVERYBODY IS ALWAYS in a rush, trying to get to some destination as quickly as possible. Is the earth circling around the sun as fast as it can to arrive somewhere? Of course not! So, why do you? You think when you get the big house you always wanted, achieve the promotion you are working hard for, find the perfect relationship, or lose an extra ten pounds, all of your worries are going to dissolve. You say things like "When I get this job" or "When I find the perfect partner."

You believe happiness is always in the future and comes from something or someone outside yourself. The illusion is that peace and harmony come when situations match your expectations. If the outcome does not match your expectations, you experience a feeling of unworthiness. If it does, you feel good for a little bit until you do not. Naturally, you chase another goal to experience this feeling again. You are working so hard to chase a feeling that is already inside yourself. The fantasy is that once you accomplish whatever goal you are pursuing, you will finally be fulfilled. It is like a fish asking another fish, "Dude, where is the water?" They cannot perceive it because they are surrounded by it. For the same reason, you are working so hard to enter the gates of heaven when, in reality, there is not even a door. You think that freedom is getting somewhere, but wherever you go, if you are not present, you will never be free.

People's favorite pastime is setting goals. A goal is a mental illusion that promises future meaning. It makes you see this moment as a means to an end. You are setting goals, achieving them, and then setting different goals again and again. This is what you call living. What is the purpose of this chasing and achieving? The tendency of the mind to search for more is natural. After all, everything in the universe is constantly moving and evolving. Yet you do not see a tree in a hurry and anxious to grow taller; it grows by being who it is. Stress happens because you are here, but your focus is on the future. The moment you create a goal, anxiety arises automatically. You worry about what can go right, what can go wrong, and how long it will take to achieve it.

There is a difference between searching and exploring. Searching comes from a place of lack. Exploring comes from a place of curiosity. When you search, this moment is never good enough. When you explore, this moment is more than enough. When you stop enjoying your daily activities for a future that has not yet happened, you miss the purpose of life. The purpose of life is not in the future.

There are three traps you fall into doing your favorite pastime:

1. Your goals are limited by how you see the world today.
2. You accomplish your goal and set another one automatically.
3. You do not achieve your goal and feel unworthy.

The goals you are chasing are based on your limited perception of how you see the world today. If you constantly learn and evolve, what means a lot to you today may not be important tomorrow. Suppose you set a goal, and then life presents a better opportunity, but you cannot see it because you are still pursuing the same old goal. Isn't that a tragedy? If you have one eye on the goal, that leaves you with just one eye to fulfill your task. This is a very inefficient way to approach life. Both eyes should be on what you are doing right now.

When you focus your energy on the future, you cannot evolve because you are not leaving room for learning. Please close your eyes and try as hard as you can to wish that everything is not as it is. Now open your eyes. Did anything change? Obviously not! You should be completely involved in doing the best you can as the world presents itself today. If you only focus on the results of your actions, you will miss the opportunity to appreciate the outcome when it arrives. You think that if you are not chasing a goal, you will never be successful, but why would this be true? If you put your full attention on whatever you are doing now, the results will follow. You want to surpass your expectations, so why have them in the first place? If you are committed to always doing the best you can, what you call your goal today will be insignificant tomorrow. You cannot experience life to the fullest if you have an eye on the future. Your stress is driven by a limited perspective and constantly changes from goal to goal.

If you accomplish your goal, two scenarios can happen. When you achieve a goal, you set another and another, like a hamster running on a wheel. This is how society tells you to become successful. You live by the misconception that your worth has something to do with your ability to accomplish goals, and if you do not achieve these goals, you are a failure. You believe that the present moment is never good enough, so you keep postponing your happiness. Eventually, you might accomplish your dream goal, the one you have been chasing for years. The kind of goal that takes a tremendous amount of energy and effort. The one you believed would lead to your eternal happiness when you achieved it. Yet, the moment you accomplish it, you feel the same as you always did. All of those feelings of inadequacy are still there. You ask yourself, *Why am I feeling the same if I accomplished my dream?* Because you cheated yourself the whole way. This is why many people, once they achieve a lot of external success like fame, wealth, or recognition, struggle to find meaning in their lives. That is why Jim Carrey famously said, "I think everybody should get rich and famous and do everything they ever dreamed of so they can see that it's not the answer." There is nothing wrong with enjoying all of the amazing experiences that this world has to offer. If you find in your heart that you want to have a particular experience, by all means, explore it. But if your activity is only a means to attain a goal, there is no way to enjoy it. You will feel hollow when you reach it. Understand that your value has nothing to do with your ability to scale the social ladder.

If you happen not to accomplish your goal, you are going to be miserable. You naturally blame yourself or worse, someone else, like your mother, the president, bad luck, your boss, or your wife. By living in this goal-setting perspective, you are losing from the start. You are playing a game you cannot win. Instead of having goals, create systems that allow you to experience and appreciate your existence.

There are three key systems you need to install:

- a system of gratitude
- a system of enjoying this moment
- a system of expansion

Gratitude is one of the most powerful tools you have at your disposal. Gratitude always brings your attention to the present moment. You will enjoy anything you do if you are fully present. Apply a system in which you train yourself to be constantly grateful. From the system of gratitude comes naturally the system of enjoying this moment. Have you ever noticed when you are enjoying the present, you are not chasing any specific goal? Actual treasures are not in the future. Each moment already has tremendous opportunities for growth. From the system of enjoying this moment comes naturally the system of expansion. You can never grow in the future; you can only grow now. Create systems, not goals. Systems always surpass goals exponentially— and without you even chasing them! You are setting a goal based on your limited perspective, and if you finally accomplish it, you will experience a feeling of meaninglessness. If you do not achieve that goal, you are going to be resentful. Goal setting is an absurd waste of time and energy. You are only chasing a goal, which is merely a slight exaggeration of something you already know. You are not letting new possibilities emerge because you are hypnotized by your goal.

So, what's left? If I have no goals, what should I do? If you want to go somewhere in your life, constantly work on yourself. Do not worry about your damn goal. You do not know what opportunities the world will present at any moment. Continuously apply a growth system in which you evolve, and you will soon realize that the goals you are chasing are so small, they now look insignificant. As Sadhguru says, "May your dreams not be fulfilled, let something you could not even dream of happen to you."

Your life should be an adventure and not an obsessive need to reach a destination. As long as you have some defined idea about the future, you cannot experience the present. Chasing a goal drives your attention to the future. If you are going to make a goal, your only goal should be to enjoy this moment. Do not sacrifice yourself for some ideal in the future. You can only experience joy at this moment. Do not fall for the trap the mind creates. When you truly understand this, life ceases to be a task and begins to be pleasurable. So, I hope you never accomplish your goals! I hope that something you cannot even imagine happens to you!

FULLY COMMITTED,
TOTALLY UNATTACHED

To understand the root of your behavior, I would like to explore what in the modern world we call a successful life. A successful life looks like acquiring things and people. But the moment you try to obtain something, no matter what it is, you always experience not having it. Your pursuit is reinforcing the fact that you do not have it in the first place.

A person looking for peace is obviously in conflict. Your quest for peace and happiness is what keeps them away from you. If you cannot be at peace at this moment, what makes you think you will be in the next one? Believing in future heaven creates present hell. Hell is living with expectations, and expectations create attachments. Attachments are the recipe for chronic dissatisfaction and nonfulfillment. Expectations are the source of unhappiness, and attachments are the source of fear. Attachments create fear of not getting what you want, getting what you do not want, or getting what you want and losing it. Attachments and expectations only exist in the mind. This is why nonattachment is discussed in every major spiritual tradition, but it is often misunderstood. Unattachment does not mean that you give up everything and move to a cave in the Himalayas. It only means that you are fully committed to what you are doing but totally unattached to the results. Expectations work like gravity. They cling to your mind and create all sorts of attachments, and it is only your expectations that create your stress.

As a culture, aspirations are focused on material attainment. The one who accumulates more toys wins. Yet have you ever noticed that money is always relatable? If tomorrow Bill Gates were to only wake up with one billion dollars, he would feel poor. Similarly, if the nice fellow who lives in the park would wake up in your shoes, he would feel like a millionaire. The idea that success is synonymous with money is like thinking safety is synonymous with wearing a bulletproof vest. A bulletproof vest can be helpful, but you can still get shot in the head! It is not about getting a specific amount of money; it is about living life to the fullest. This is why Chuck Palahniuk wrote in *Fight Club*, "We buy things we don't need with money we don't have to impress people we don't like."

People are frustrated and exhausted because they are pursuing contradictory goals. Nothing in the outside world can possibly give you eternal fulfillment because everything around you is constantly changing. Society tells you that if you go to school, get a job, buy a house, or have a family, you will be eternally fulfilled. The contradiction is that you are trained to live for the future, yet you are always in the present. If a sense of inadequacy drives the seed of your behavior, it does not matter what you accomplish. It will never go away. Living in contradiction is exhausting. Anxiety happens because the mind is always saying, "I want."

Isn't it funny how people work to retire? You keep working, doing something you do not like, to keep on living, so you can keep doing something you do not like. Do you see the trap that you are in? If you work in order to retire, you are treating the present as a means to an end. If you are not enjoying your present, I guarantee you will not enjoy retirement either because you are training your mind to always look for happiness in the future. Your belief in future heaven is why you tolerate present hell. And hell is only in your imagination, so get out of there. Do not waste any more time in this trap. In fact, I hope you never retire! I hope you will always find projects that excite and challenge you. Working to retire is a goal-oriented life that is leading nowhere. The way you get everything you want is by realizing you already have it.

Do you not see the search for happiness makes you feel like you lack it in the first place? The urge to be happy is natural, but the means you are using are misleading. Happiness is always in some other place or some other moment. It is always in the past, in "the good old days," or in an imaginary future. The past gives you an identity, and the future gives you a promise of fulfillment. Neither one exists. Both are an illusion. You are willing to sacrifice your present opportunity for joy for an imaginary reward in the future. How crazy is this? When you live life merely for the results of your actions, your sacrifices end up being in vain because you are wasting the only thing you truly have: this moment. Have you ever questioned why it is called the present? Because the present is a gift! Enjoy it.

Happiness does not depend on any person or circumstance. When you place it in something outside yourself, you live as a slave to external circumstances, scared that someone can take it away. Tethering your happiness to an external object like money or possessions, a person like your girlfriend or husband, or a circumstance such as a job is a recipe for dissatisfaction because you are constantly fearful and hypervigilant. You lose a lot of energy protecting whatever you tie your happiness to. This does not mean that you cannot enjoy your possessions, relationships, or work. On the contrary, you will appreciate them more because you are not wasting any energy protecting them. Have you ever been in a needy relationship? If you have, you can confidently say it is not the most enjoyable one. Neediness creates anxiety and prevents you from thoroughly enjoying whatever you think you need. What you are truly saying when you look for someone's approval is this: "Your view of me is more important than my own opinion." Neediness accomplishes the opposite of the desired result. With a goal-setting attitude, you pursue objects, people, or circumstances with a sense of neediness. A sense of neediness is the fastest way to keep them away from you. You compete when you tie your happiness to something external and act defensively because you believe someone can take it away. Being defensive blocks growth. If you are defensive, you will never be free.

The US Constitution mentions "life, liberty, and the pursuit of happiness." If you are pursuing happiness, you are never going to find it! True happiness happens when you are not looking for it. You do not need to seek it because happiness is your nature. Your unhappiness is totally made up. If you look at kids, they are happy by nature. Something has to happen for them to experience unhappiness. Now, as an adult, you are living the other way around. Someone or something has to make you happy; if not, you are unhappy. Your constant desire for accomplishment creates expectations. And it is only your expectations that are blocking you from experiencing happiness. Where do your expectations come from anyway? If you look at them, they always come in comparison to other people. They are not even yours! They make you anxious, competitive, and jealous. That's why Theodore Roosevelt said, "Comparison is the thief of joy." Searching for happiness is like trying to bite your own teeth. In other words, it is pointless. Everything you do with expectations blinds you. The moment you let go of your expectations is the moment you experience freedom.

When you do anything as a means to an end, you tend to do it unwillingly. The only difference between joy and suffering is if you do something willingly or not. If your attention is only on the results, you are never going to enjoy whatever you do. Instead of treating the present as a means to an end, be autotelic. *Autotelic* means doing an activity for its own sake. When you do something you enjoy, the reward is the activity. It is like the guy who uses the stock market to make money versus the guy who loves playing it. The activity they are doing is the same, but their experience is worlds apart. If the market goes down, the first guy has a panic attack, but the second uses this situation to sharpen his skill set. With whom would you rather invest your money? And who would you rather be: the one who treats the present as a means to an end or the one who is autotelic?

The most powerful way to approach life is to be fully committed but totally unattached. Fully committed in the present and totally unattached to the future. When you are fully committed, you do the task that presents itself to the best of your ability. When you do the best you can, you can confidently detach yourself from the results and remain open to any possibility that life presents. When you are totally unattached, you allow life to surprise you.

Stop missing opportunities because you happen to be hypnotized by a specific outcome. Have you ever noticed when you are most powerful? Definitely not when your mind is making up scenarios that have not yet happened. Being present makes you powerful! When your mind is wandering around, you miss the chance to create the life you want. To be fully committed and totally unattached is to accept everything as it is right now. Can you find peace regardless of what is happening in your life? If you cannot, you are creating resistance. You cannot experience your full capabilities if you are resisting this moment. Resistance blocks creativity. Being in harmony with everything as it is right now brings freedom. Only from this space can you enter a world of creativity and create the life you want. Get rid of the fear of failure. Get rid of your anxieties about success. Stop driving your life by pressing on the brakes. Just be fully committed and totally unattached.

True success is when you are completely free, totally at peace, regardless of what is happening. If you focus on being the broadest version of yourself, it does not matter what situation life presents. You do not avoid anything because you can deal with everything. You act accordingly, not defensively. Free yourself from expectations. Adopt Michael Singer's formula for success: "Do whatever is put in front of you with all your heart and soul without regard for personal results. Do the work as though it was given to you by the universe itself—because it was."

Perfect action comes when you play the game of life entirely, very intensely, with all your awareness, focus, and heart, but with complete detachment of the outcome. Be fully present without being afraid of what will happen next. With this approach, life will take you to places you cannot even imagine. Temporary pleasures depend on things; happiness does not. True happiness is spontaneous and effortless. Say it aloud: "I am in harmony with the ways things are, and I am fully committed to the version of myself I want to experience. I am fully committed and totally unattached."

LIVING TO BE SUCCESSFUL IS LIKE SWIMMING TO FIND WATER

HAVE YOU EVER QUESTIONED WHY YOU WANT TO BE SUCCESSFUL so badly? What is success anyway? It has so many different meanings to so many different people. If you do not question and define it on your own, you will pursue someone else's definition of success. That does not sound like a fun life to me. Questions control your focus. They create the opportunity for an answer to happen. Look at the word *question*; it has "quest" in it. Any quest always begins with a question.

People always ask how to become successful, but they do not even know what success is. Isn't this strange? What kind of questions are you asking? How to be successful is a question that comes out of fear. Questions that come out of fear have limited answers, and they close the mind. Questions that come out of curiosity have unlimited potential, and they open the mind to new possibilities. Living to be successful is like swimming to find water. In other words, it is absurd.

Wanting to be successful is reinforcing the fact that you are not. You live as if this moment is never good enough—like you are missing something. You think if it were not for your nose,

15

job, boss, bank account, and so on, then everything would be okay. You perceive the world based on whatever you think you lack. If you are insecure about your weight when you see a skinny person, you think she is enlightened because she is thin. Your perception of lack is making imaginary projections that you end up experiencing as your reality. Lack only comes when you chase someone else's definition of success. Have you ever questioned why you were born in this body? In this family? In this country? Why are there certain things you are attracted to? Your existence has so many mysteries that to focus on some else's is simply foolish. Questions of growth transform bad situations into opportunities. Depending on what you ask, you will experience a situation as either a possibility or a problem. Even if something "bad" happens, instead of closing your mind, ask growth questions: What can I learn from this experience? How can I make it useful? When you do, you stop perceiving life as a problem and start experiencing it as an opportunity. Before you make any decision, no matter how big or small, it is essential to take a moment and ask, "Is my decision aligned with the version of myself I want to experience?" The questions you ask are telling you where you focus your attention. When you upgrade your questions, you upgrade your life like the apps on your phone.

Your intentions are always driven by the questions you ask. Questions about fear create *instrument goals*, and questions about curiosity enable a holistic life. An instrument goal is when you treat your activity as a means to an end—something you "should" do to get somewhere else. For example, if you only go to college to get a job, you are using your education as a means to an end. In other words, it is an instrument goal. Instead of going to college to make new friends, learn about different subjects, and be curious, you are only going to get somewhere that only exists in your imagination. You cannot enjoy anything if you are trying to get somewhere else.

If you use the present as a means to the future, the present loses its significance. When you chase instrument goals, you chase someone else's definition of success. Instrument goals are the ones society tells you that you need to achieve to be happy. Look at your life and notice if you are doing something to get someplace else. Many people use relationships as instrument goals. They enter relationships not to feel lonely. Instead of being with someone they genuinely admire, they are with someone to avoid their feelings. Their approach comes from a place of lack. If a means to an end becomes your focus, you missed the point. Please understand you do not have to go to college to be successful, you do not have to get married to be happy, and you do not have to be on a diet to be healthy. So how should you approach life? Holistically!

A holistic approach does not focus on the situation but your reaction. When you control your inner state, it does not matter where you are or what life throws at you. If you think about it, what you really want is to be in an exquisite loving relationship, learn and express your interests, and have constant challenges to grow. By being frequently grateful, surrounded by love, and constantly learning, you experience what you are looking for.

There are always more things you can be grateful for than things you can complain about. For example, if you have a flat tire, instead of putting your attention in complaining, better use this experience to be grateful that you have a car in the first place. By constantly being grateful, you are teaching your mind acceptance while eliminating the habit of complaining. Acceptance means that you willingly accept what this moment asks you to do. Without gratitude, enjoying life is impossible. Gratitude is your power—use it! Do not let any person or situation take it away. As Rumi said, "Gratitude is the wine for the soul, go on, get drunk!" Every morning when you wake up, say to life, "Show me what you have, and watch how I respond—always grateful!"

You can always be surrounded by love by being love. Love is the feeling of unity with the rest of existence. Yet sometimes, you forget the laws. The first law is you have an unlimited supply inside yourself. Love is what you truly are. So, do not be tacky—give it to everyone! The second law is that the more love you give, the more you experience it. For example, when you take an Uber, you can secretly wish the driver to have a day full of light. By sending the driver love, you are reminding yourself you are the source of it. Love is your power—use it! Do not let any person or situation take it away. When you wake up, remember you do not need anyone or anything to give you the love you already are.

You can always be curious and constantly learning. Remember, it all starts with growth questions. The universe gives you, in each moment, learning opportunities. However, are you receptive, or are you still living in your mind, reacting to your thoughts, and missing the opportunity the world is trying to teach you? People say that they are waiting for a sign, but the signals are all around. They are just walking blindfolded by expectations and fears. Curiosity takes away the blindfold and sees everything as a learning tool. Stop judging experiences as good or bad and learn from them. In my personal life, I learn the most when I am in silence—observing the world around me without any judgment and my thoughts without clinging to them. Curiosity is your power. Use it! Do not let any person or situation take it away. Every morning when you wake up, say to life, "I am curious and open to learn whatever lessons you have for me today."

When you approach life holistically, you develop yourself daily. When you begin to explore yourself, life becomes more fun and less rigid. If the means do not make you happy, I guarantee you the ends will not either. A *holistic mentality* enables your powers, and instrument goals disable them. It does not matter where you are or who you are hanging out with. If you maintain your holistic approach, you always enjoy life. You stop chasing other people's definitions of success and begin exploring your life by your own definition. Many people dream about winning the lottery, but let me tell you, if you win the lottery today but do not apply your holistic mindset, your life will be impossible to enjoy. Whatever happens, remember always to be grateful, surrounded by love, and constantly learning.

WHATEVER YOU ARE SCARED
OF IS BASED ON A LIE

THE NATURE OF LIFE IS UNCERTAINTY; EVERYTHING IS ALWAYS changing. Cells in your body are dying as you read this page. On the other hand, new healthy cells are being born. Your cells divide between two and three trillion times every single day. This means your brain, organs, skin, and the rest of your body regenerates itself constantly. Yet, you are not stressed because cells in your body are dying. The universe works in the same way; it is always in flux. The earth is rotating; countries are altering political ideas; a new team is winning the Super Bowl, and even what you like and dislike changes all the time. The circumstances of your life are changing from moment to moment. Nothing ever stays stagnant. Uncertainty is the fundamental law of the universe. Trying to find certainty in a universe where everything is constantly changing is not only a waste of time but also exhausting because you are fighting against nature.

The priority of the human brain is keeping you alive. The brain predicts and protects based on past behaviors and experiences to ensure your survival. It is constantly scanning for potential threats in order to avoid them. The human predicament is that while the universe is always changing, your brain is trying to find certainty at the same time. The desire for security is the experiencing of insecurity. You are looking at each moment with contact lenses of the past: vigilant, worried, and protective.

The human condition is always fighting two opposite forces: constant change versus trying to find security. The contradiction is the desire for safety with the reality of change. The result is exhaustion from this constant battle. True freedom is recognizing that you do not know what will happen and being okay with it. The more you invite uncertainty into your life, the more secure you will feel. Strange paradox. Fear is an anticipation of a future that has not yet happened. It only exists when the mind tries to find security in an uncertain universe. Fear always comes from a model you have inside your head of how things should be. No wonder why you are so tired; it is an exhausting way to live. What are you scared of losing? What model of how things should be are you holding onto?

Your mind is operating from a program of protection. Fear is only a symptom that something is happening against the way you think it should be. Whenever fear comes, notice where it is coming from. What mental boundaries are making you experience fear? My work is to help you get out of survival mechanisms to access a world of possibilities.

Instead of wasting energy protecting your mental boundaries, which are fear-based boundaries, use that energy to create the life you want. In the modern world, you deal with fears and anxieties that do not threaten your survival. The problem is that your body does not know the difference between a real threat and the ones you make up.

So, let's suppose your boss tells you he needs to talk to you in private in his office. Immediately, you start thinking, *What did I do wrong? Am I getting fired? How am I going to tell my family? How am I going to pay rent?* Your body's chemistry starts to change. The sympathetic nervous system is activated, releasing stress hormones and putting your body into a fight-or-flight response. Your heart starts pumping faster, your digestion begins to slow, and your pupils start dilating. Your entire body chemistry changed just because your boss told you that he wants to talk to you. Why would you give someone the keys to the laboratory of your body? And do you know for a fact that you are getting fired? Maybe you are getting the promotion you always wanted. It does not matter whether you are getting fired or promoted. Your mind is making you experience now what you are scared of facing. The key to living in harmony is accepting the way things are now. Understand that everything is temporary. This will allow you to experience some freedom. From this space, you can decide if you want to change something in your life or not.

The first step in welcoming uncertainty is acknowledging the human predicament in which you live. When you see that it is in your human nature, the constant battle of survival versus the reality of change, you can start transcending it. You waste an absurd amount of energy trying to predict and protect yourself from self-generated threats. You probably know someone who spends months planning a vacation, and as soon as they arrive, they start checking their flight back and when they return home, say, "I need a vacation from my vacation." This happens because you are constantly fighting uncertainty. You want to predict everything that will happen in your life. And because it is impossible, you end up needing vacations from your vacations!

Welcoming uncertainty creates space in your brain because you stop using its energy for protection. The more you try to control a situation, the more fear you feel. Consequently, the more you let go, the more trust you experience. By embracing uncertainty, you eliminate fear. Fearlessness is one of the most powerful ways to approach life. Fearlessness comes by itself when you realize that there is nothing to be afraid of, when you see fear as your own creation.

In the *Bhagavad Gita*, fearlessness is described as a divine state called *Abhaya*. With less fear and more awareness, your consciousness expands. Any decision made out of fear makes you feel anxious and paralyzes you. Even scientific studies say that your brain cannot access its full capabilities when you are afraid. In other words, fear makes you dumber. Where did these fears come from anyway? Are they contributing to your life? Are they necessary? Are they real? By asking these questions, you can see that fear only exists in your imagination. If you can transcend your fears, you can control your life. Letting go of your fears is the first step in creating the abundant life you have always dreamed of.

Fear is a funny creature. It only exists in your mind. Whatever you are scared of is based on a lie. Let's suppose you lived in the time society thought the earth was flat. What would you be afraid of? Naturally, you would fear falling into the void. Suddenly someone told you that the earth was round, and instantly your fear of falling disappeared completely. What changed? The planet remained the same, and the people remained the same; the only thing that changed was your perspective, and all the fear instantly disappeared.

Fear is like if you were to go on a vacation, and when you arrive at your hotel room, while everything is dark, you think you see a snake on the floor. You race out of the room, find the manager, and say, "There is a snake in my room!"

When the manager turns on the lights, you see the snake was only a rope. If you turn on the light of your fears, you will laugh because you will see that your mind was playing tricks on you. Fear prevents you from growing because it paralyzes you. Fear, as they say, is only *false evidence appearing real*. As Michael Jordan says, "Limits, like fears, are often just an illusion." You have exaggerated your fears. You are looking at them as if they are a snake, but in reality, they are only a rope. There is nothing to be afraid of. All you need to do is turn on the light of awareness. Fear does not have power; it only has the power you give it. Look at what is making you afraid. Do not try to avoid it. Do not attempt to repress it. Just look at it. Turn on the light, and the fear will disappear automatically.

Fear is the mother of all negative emotions. Her kids are worrying, uneasy, tense, depressed, nervous, anxious, and lack confidence. All of these come from fear. If you can eliminate the root of the problem, all of the leaves die automatically. Fear and worry always come together. They act as a couple. They hold hands and settle down inside your mind. Once they are in, they start to destroy their competition: creativity, joy, laughter, and compassion. The worst part about this destructive partnership is that they give nothing in return while they demand and take a tremendous amount of energy. Their whole tendency is to suppress progress.

Nobody has ever accomplished anything by living in the perception of fear and worry. Have you ever noticed that fear disappears every time you are joyful? Fear can only come when you are not enjoying the present moment. Fear and worry destroy the possibility of celebrating life. You are not afraid of the unknown. You are only scared of losing what you know. Defeat fear by realizing that everything you are scared of is based on a lie.

FEAR IS SO BORING

YOUR LIFE IS YOUR UNIVERSE, AND IT IS CREATED BASED UPON your perceptions. You create your reality by how you perceive yourself, how you see the people around you, and how you relate to your surroundings. Have you ever noticed that whenever you have a perception of fear, life is so boring? You do not experience anything new or exciting. Fear always makes predictable decisions. Decisions made out of fear tend to lead you nowhere. They do not allow you to investigate new ways to experience yourself, new directions you can go, and new adventures you could enjoy. Fear makes you want to hold on to familiar behaviors in your life. Fear is the enemy of growth. So, why are you hanging out with it?

Fear is something that arises naturally under certain circumstances. What would you do if it was snowing outside? You would accept the environment that you are in and put on a jacket. Similarly, it is very natural to be afraid. The only way it can disappear is when you accept it. When you repress or reject fear, you end up being afraid of being afraid. Funny because running from fear is the definition of it. If you have fear, you have fear—what is the problem? Whenever fear arises, acknowledge it, like the natural phenomena that it is, and remember it is something momentary that is only passing by. So, why take it seriously?

Acting from a place of fear only creates more fear. Do not move as fear tells you to. Move as curiosity dictates, as joy wants you to. Go wherever love takes you. Also, why are you moving through life so seriously? Start moving laughingly.

There are two types of fear: *physical* and *psychological*. Physical fear arises when your survival is threatened. Like, if you are exiting the subway and someone pulls a knife on you because they want to steal your wallet. Your body activates a system that releases adrenaline. It sends all your energy into your muscles; this is called the *sympathetic nervous system*. This system is very useful under these conditions because you can run faster to get away (for the record, my recommendation if this situation happens is to give the wallet to the robber and move on with your day; maybe life is teaching you how not to become attached to things). The other type of fear is psychological. This fear only exists in your imagination. Psychological fear is the one that keeps you awake at night. The one that takes an enormous amount of energy without giving anything in return. Psychological fear is what Buddha referred to when he said, "Fear does not prevent death; it prevents life."

You are only afraid of anticipation. If tomorrow you were to go skydiving, tonight you would be scared of jumping. The next day, when you are on the plane, you would still be afraid, but the fear disappears when you jump. Similarly, fear disappears when you look at the root cause. You usually look at the circumstance instead of what it is revealing. You are not getting rid of the problem—only the symptoms. You end up avoiding situations instead of transcending your fears.

For example, if you are acting possessive, treating the symptoms would look like trying to control your spouse. Instead, if you look at the root cause of your behavior, you may find that you feel a sense of unworthiness. Acting possessively, which is fear-based behavior, is only revealing what you need to work on internally. Some helpful questions you can ask yourself include: What am I scared of losing? Why am I reacting with fear to this situation? What is fear preventing me from experiencing? What is fear trying to teach me?

Fear is the guide that tells you what area of your life you need more awareness. Some default settings that come from being human are the fear of inadequacy, not-enough-ness, abandonment, and loss. Usually, when you are scared, you panic, and you start to anticipate outcomes that have not yet happened. When you react, you miss the chance to know what is creating your stress. Instead of classifying fear as something negative, use it. Once you can stare fear in the face, you get to know yourself. A great tool you can use is to ask, Is this true? Is it true that somehow I'm not enough? You will find out that your fears are only opinions and not facts.

Have you ever noticed that fear is always in relation to something else? Fear is never an isolated thing. If you really think about it, fear has nothing to do with you. You are afraid of not getting what you want, making mistakes, losing people, possessions, status, and so on. All of these fears are about a model you have. Fear arises in relation to your attachments. The degree of how attached you are to losing something is in correlation to the degree to which you are not free. What would happen if you let go of these beliefs? How many fears are you a slave to?

Everything in the universe is constantly moving, evolving, and changing. So, by definition, everything is temporary. You start to experience stress when you forget this natural law and try to cling to temporary things. Attachment to momentary objects becomes your source of fear. It is like when you go on vacation and stay at a beautiful hotel. You enjoy the pool, the restaurant, the sheets, and the service because you know you will leave. This makes you present because you want to take full advantage of your vacation. It's funny how the mind works. Even when you are in your ideal situation, you are afraid that this event is going to end. And it will! That is part of the fun. Your attitude toward all experiences and possessions should be like when you visit an excellent hotel. You should welcome everything that comes into your life, knowing that it will go away. This makes you appreciate the uniqueness of each moment. Welcome everything with an open heart, allowing it to come and go as it has to. Instead of clinging and being afraid, you are grateful that you got to experience something—even just for a little bit. And remember, fear and greed are one.

Acknowledging that everything is temporary, why would you stay in your comfort zone and not try new things? Why not take that risk you always wanted to take? You are going to die anyway. Why not invite that girl you always liked to dinner? Or start your own business? Get this, the experience of risk you feel is relative to your perception of inadequacy. For example, if you have a lot of confidence and you are an extrovert, asking someone out will not feel like a risky situation. But if you are timid and shy, asking will feel like you are risking your whole life. The chances of getting a date are the same: fifty-fifty, yes or no. Maybe the girl has a boyfriend, perhaps she likes the same books as you do, or maybe she's the love of your life.

Similar is the feeling of risk a housewife experiences when buying a stock. She can feel as if she is gambling her life away. But for the stock trader, buying a stock is like eating lunch. The risk of the stock's value going up or down is the same. However, the experience is entirely different. The perception of risk is internal; it is not external. If you understand that your perception of risk itself is limited to your insecurities, you can take the wildest risk with ease and calmness.

The moment you see risk as an opportunity is the moment you crave it. When you move in any direction, the outcome does not matter because you evolve along the way into your next adventure. The most significant risk is not taking one. Not doing something is doing something. Replacing fear with curiosity opens the door of your mind to the unknown. To embrace the unknown is to transcend your fears. Jump out of the plane and watch how fear disappears. If you do not get what you want, that is as interesting as if you do. Did you ever notice that? So, why be afraid?

Trust and fear cannot coexist. Do not fight your fear. Do not repress it—just bring more energy into trust. Attention is the food; give it to trust. Once fear is gone, you can step into any situation you want to experience. You can take any risk you want to take because you realize there is no risk at all.

Jim Carrey said, "You can fail at what you don't want, so you might as well take a chance on doing what you love." His father was a talented comedian, but he was too afraid to pursue it and ended up working as an accountant. He got fired anyway years later. There are no guarantees in life. Taking the "safe bet" does not mean you are not taking any risks. It only means the risks you are taking are in accordance with your fears and not according to your dreams.

31

RESISTANCE IS SUFFERING

HAVE YOU EVER NOTICED HOW YOU TALK TO YOURSELF, YOUR clients, your friends, your family, and strangers on the subway? I guarantee in most of these conversations, you think: "He should not have done that," "I wish she did this instead," or "Why did I do this?" There is always another way you believe people should behave. Or you should have acted differently than the way you did. Everyone is doing the best they can with their current level of awareness. If everyone, including you, acted precisely how you wanted them to, no one would be able to grow and have a better understanding of themselves. Also, life would be pretty boring.

You create resistance when you do not accept the way things are. Resistance is only a belief you have about how everything should be; it is not even real. Your mind is totally making it up. First, you are implying that you know how things are supposed to occur. It is like you start pointing at the sky and screaming, "The sun should rise from the west to the east instead of from east to west!" How crazy does that sound? Any rational person would tell you this is how the sun rises. Your screaming will not change the direction in which the earth rotates. They would probably put you in a mental hospital for trying to change the sun's direction. By assuming how everything should occur and how everyone, including yourself, should behave, you do the same thing. Your resistance to the past will not change the present. It only creates suffering. Next time your mind starts telling you that things are not supposed to be the way they are, tell your mind that you will put it in a mental hospital.

Secondly, your nonacceptance in this moment creates side effects: guilt, regret, anger, frustration, and anxiety. Resisting what is eliminates any possibility of kindness to yourself and others. Anxiety only happens when you resist life's events. Resistance is the activity in which you exchange a tremendous amount of energy for a tremendous amount of stress. In other words, it is bad business. Resistance denies space for creativity.

Thinking that you know how things should occur is ridiculous. Your rational mind cannot predict the future. There are too many variables. More importantly, why do you want to predict your life instead of living it? Your struggle about how you see the past is not allowing you to move forward. Do you believe you are a victim of circumstances? Are you resisting the way things are right now? Say what Deepak Chopra says: "I know that this moment is as it should be because the whole universe is as it should be … When you struggle against this moment, you are struggling against the entire universe." Eliminate the shoulds from your life, and the whole world will appear differently.

How would you respond if you got fired from your job? You would initially feel fear, which will transform into anger. First, you would start blaming life because it is so unfair. You are the unlucky bastard who cannot catch a break. Second, you would begin blaming everyone around you, including your boss and coworkers. Lastly, you start judging yourself. All the emotions you already carry inside, like feelings of inadequacy, will show up, and they come on steroids.

You do not know what you are going to do. Your illusion of security is gone. At that moment, you truly believe you are a victim of life, but why are you resisting what's happening? Why do you think this is so terrible after all? Do you know the complete picture of your life? A little time passes, and you decide to take your bucket list trip to Argentina. You always wanted to go, but you were too busy. Here, your attitude has no resistance, and you are fully accepting what's going on, which makes you radiant. Because you come from a place of curiosity and joy—and not resistance or fear—you attract the girl of your dreams. Are you still upset and angry because you got fired? Are you still complaining that what happened to you was unfair? Or, are you grateful that you were laid off? Something you saw as unjust is now a blessing. You could not see it before, but now you can. Life works like this. Blessings often come in disguise. Opportunities appear camouflaged as misfortune. Life was removing you from a place where you were stuck.

Usually, you believe you are your job, your relationships, or your possessions. So, when you lose your job, someone steals your phone, or someone breaks up with you, it is only a reminder you are not those things. Jobs, relationships, and possessions come and go, yet here you are! Life made you take a risk that you would never have taken without a push. Remember, you only lose what you try to keep; you cannot lose what you give.

Whenever something that seems negative happens to you, there is always a lesson hidden in it. Seen from a higher perspective, situations are always positive. Suffering is only pointing out an area in your life where you need to grow. Suffering is pointless when you do not learn anything from it.

The moment I learned how to use my suffering, I felt like I was cheating. Whenever something negative happens to me, instead of reacting and complaining, it actually excites me because it shows where I'm still stuck. I do not embrace these situations in a masochistic way—I do not want negative things to happen—but when they do, it excites me. I know they are the perfect chance to become a more powerful human being.

How many things happened to you years ago that you perceived as negative, and you ended up suffering unnecessarily? Today, you can acknowledge that you went through these "negative" circumstances for your evolution. Were they really bad after all? How much energy did you waste by resisting, blaming, getting angry, feeling scared, and trying to control the outcome? If you watch what is going on without getting emotionally attached, your life improves instantly. Peter Crone said it beautifully: "What happened, happened, and it couldn't happen any other way, you know why? Because it didn't!" Next time something happens that you perceive as negative, remember that you are not a victim of life. Life is always taking care of you in mysterious ways.

Your resistance to your emotions and feelings generates your suffering. Attachments create expectations and dependencies. In other words, they create suffering. Your resistance to the past and anticipation about the future makes you suffer. But where is the past? Only in your memory. Do you remember what you did twenty-three days ago? Your whole day? Every minute of it?

Of course not! So, how can you trust your memory? Memories are no more than selections. If you have no memory, where is the problem? Do not live by the misconception that memory is intelligence. Memory has its purpose, but it is not intelligence. Your phone can store a lot of music, but it cannot compose a song. Use your memory without allowing your memory to use you. You never look at the past. You always look at the present with the lens of a past memory. And also, where is the future? Do you know what is going to happen in precisely eight minutes? Obviously not! So, why are you wasting your time trying to predict the unpredictable? It is only your mind that makes you anxious and unhappy. As Dr. Jordan Peterson said, "The reason you have a memory is not to remember the past, but to not do the same stupid things in the future."

The only way you can access your full intelligence is to stop resisting the past and stop predicting the future. Only in the present can you find freedom. Only in the present can you be creative. Accept everything as it is right now, and from that space of nonresistance, use your full intelligence to create the life you want.

Zen Buddhism teaches two principles for awakening: *kesho* and *satori*. Kesho is enlightenment through suffering; Satori is sudden enlightenment. If you are suffering right now, instead of resisting, use it! Grow through it—do not miss this chance. If you are not suffering, get into the richness of this moment. Do not let the mind wander. You can get enlightened without the necessity of suffering. The cool thing is that you can use your sorrow or joy for awakening if you stop complaining. When you complain, you miss the chance. Whether it is a bad driver, a lazy barista, or the store sold out of avocados, you need to realize when you complain about anything, you are actually complaining about the whole universe.

There is a yogic story about two monks walking in the desert. As they approached a river, they came across a young lady with no shoes. She asked the monks if they could help her cross to the other side.

The older monk, without hesitation, carried her on his shoulders and helped her cross to the other side of the river.

The two monks kept walking in silence for another four hours until they arrived at their destination.

Once they arrived, the younger monk, with an angry face, said, "What were you thinking? We made a vow that we would never touch a woman!"

The older monk calmly responded, "I dropped her four hours ago. You, on the other hand, are still carrying her."

Resistance serves no purpose. Emotional suffering comes from the models of how you think the universe *should* work. Stop yelling at the sun to rotate the other way around. Stop doing business with resistance and get into the enterprise of acceptance.

The experience of suffering is in relationship to your attachments. If you are hiking a beautiful mountain with the most amazing view while carrying a backpack full of rocks, no matter how in shape you are, you will start getting tired until, finally, you are utterly exhausted. At the same time, your awareness will be on your back and shoulders instead of on the stunning view. You will not even notice if a rainbow appears in the sky. This is how you live if you carry any emotional resistance. You are still holding on to things that happened years ago. Stop carrying the backpack of fear, anger, sadness, resentment, and disappointment. Let them go. They no longer serve you. Always remember that resistance and suffering are one.

THE ONLY PROBLEM
YOU HAVE IS BELIEVING
YOU HAVE ONE

PEOPLE BELIEVE LIFE IS ABOUT SOLVING PROBLEMS. YOU TALK about your issues all the time with friends, family, and you may even go to a therapist. No matter who you talk to or how much time you spend thinking about them, as long as you believe you have a problem, you will always imagine there is something wrong with this moment. If you think something is wrong, you feel the need to do something in order to fix it. Wanting to improve this moment creates resistance. And your refusal to accept the way things are creates suffering. Your resistance is making you believe that you have a problem. Why are you suffering? Why do you make life into a problem to be solved? You only think you have a problem because you are looking at a situation from a fixed point of view.

Situations are happening all the time, from moment to moment. When you do not know how to handle a particular circumstance, you instantly call it a problem. There are no problems in life. None. The "problems" you pay so much attention to are just events happening. It is in the way you frame those events that make you experience them as a problem.

Anything that life throws at you, you can see it as a possibility or as a problem. What is a problem for you, someone else may interpret as a possibility. The way things are might not be ideal, things might not be as you want them to be, but nevertheless, they are what they are. To get out of a situation, you need to radically accept where you are right now. Be aware because the more you talk about your problems, the more you reinforce that you have one. Problems only exist in the mind, not in reality. If you look at life as a problem to be solved, you will see them everywhere. But if you see life as pure possibility, you will see opportunities everywhere. When you look at life through the lens of "something is wrong," you automatically put yourself in a state of resistance. The sense of misery is not in the circumstance itself; it is in your interpretation and response to it. If you understand this, you stop blaming the situation and start focusing on your reaction. Your mindset is the determinant factor in how you experience life.

Whether you have a problem in life or not depends on your attitude. The moment you are all right with everything, everything is all right with you. Instead of focusing on solving problems, you should focus on dissolving them. For dissolving your concerns, ask yourself, What limited belief do I have that makes me perceive this situation as a problem? If you ask the right questions, you can get to the root of your subconscious limitations. When a problem arises, you tend to ask, What should I do about it? How can I fix it? If you focus on a solution, you are giving your power away because you are missing the chance to see what it is revealing inside. You are implying that something outside is responsible for your reaction. Instead, use this situation as an instrument of growth.

The next time you believe you have a problem, ask growth questions: What part of me is feeling concerned? Why do I perceive this as a threat? How can I learn from this? What limited belief inside me is making me react? Problems do not need to be solved; they need to be understood. Just be careful because whatever you judge or try to control, you cannot understand. A problem grows and grows when you resist it, but it disappears when you understand it.

It is only your ideas about how things should be that creates a problem in your mind. If you are suffering, it is because you are trying to force some specific outcome. Problems are simply a lack of understanding about the limiting beliefs you carry inside. For example, when you are stubborn, you tend to blame the other person for not understanding. But you are not trying to understand them either. It is a pretty foolish approach, is it not? Trying to fix the problem looks like trying to make other people wrong. Anger is only the vehicle that is revealing where you are not free. Anger is a symptom of a sense of inadequacy. No matter who you are talking to, if you do not understand what makes you react, you will always be stubborn and insecure. If you focus on yourself instead of what the other person is doing, you can discover your subconscious limitations, understand them, and dissolve them. Once you dissolve your problems, you realize they never really were in the first place. The day you understand that you are enough, I guarantee you will stop making others wrong.

Have you noticed that problems only come up when you think about them? When you are not thinking about them, where are they? All problems are psychological. The only thing that is happening is that your mind is working against you. It is anticipating imaginary situations that have not yet happened. If you are going to imagine something, at least imagine things that make you feel joyful. Nothing can trouble you but your imagination. When you label any situation as a problem, your mind closes automatically. Your thoughts, ideas, and actions act defensively against self-generated threats. You can only access a world of creativity when you are in a state of radical acceptance. The universal law is that what you focus on grows. If you are putting all your energy into your problems, guess what your next thought is going to be? Have you ever noticed you talk so much about your issues and so little about your dreams? The secret of creation is this: Accept everything as it is right now, and from that space, focus all your awareness on your dreams and not on your problems.

The root of almost every problem is that you do not feel worthy of love. There is a difference between analysis and witnessing. Western psychology focuses on analysis. It says you have to think about your problem, find its cause, and go into its history—even back to when you were a kid. This is absurd! How can a thought stop another thought? How can the mind analyze itself? Why are you measuring yourself by the criteria of your thoughts? You are creating the belief that something is wrong with you. There is nothing wrong with you. You are not broken. There is nothing to be fixed. The only thing that is happening is that fears and insecurity dust the lens through which you see the world. Analysis is a vicious circle because you never realize who is the one who is watching the problem. It is only the mind trying to analyze the mind. Ancient Eastern knowledge says the opposite—that no problem is severe. A problem arises because you identified with it. Witnessing creates space between you and your problems. The key to solving any problem is to realize there are no problems. Analysis attempts to explain the dust, and witnessing removes it from your life.

Patanjali, the father of Raja yoga, teaches that indifference is the best weapon against any negative situation. Lack of attention dissolves the problem. For example, if your boyfriend dumped you, you will naturally be sad, angry, and resentful. When you are stuck in your mind, you believe you are these emotions. However, when you witness them, they lose their power. It is not about rejecting these emotions. It is about looking, accepting, and letting them pass through you. Denying or ignoring these feelings is a form of nonacceptance that manifests as a problem later. Why not just accept and use them as instruments for growth? It is only your attachment that is making you suffer. If you accept what is, the suffering disappears right away.

Neem Karoli Baba, an enlightened guru, used to say, "Give up your anger. Don't analyze it. Don't even look at it—just give it up!"

Patanjali and Neem Karoli Baba, two of the most respected spiritual masters, teach to stop giving so much attention to your "problems," or better, dissolve them and realize they do not exist. There are many illnesses of the mind, but there is only one cure: Wake up!

Let's analyze a scenario in which you can transform a problem into a possibility: You are at a dinner party with your girlfriend's friends. Suddenly, you start to get annoyed and want to go home.

You say, "Let's go home," but your girl is enjoying herself. She says, "Let's stay another thirty minutes." You have two options: You can resist the situation by staring at the clock and counting the seconds until you can go home. Looking at your watch does not make the time go any faster; it usually works the other way around. Or you can accept the situation you are in, which creates many curious options. You can start listening to the table conversation. You can watch the person you love enjoying herself and notice her body language. You might even start a conversation with the person next to you and learn something new. Next thing you know, two hours have passed, and you go home with a big smile.

When you are in the present moment, you have unlimited possibilities. When you are in resistance, you only have one, suffering. When you expand your awareness, you change the energy in the room. Instead of being the person who is anxious and resistant, you become present and enjoyable. As Michael Beckwith says, "The problems you have in one state of consciousness do not exist in a higher level of awareness." If you raise your level of awareness, you realize that all problems are only illusions. Life is not about solving problems; it is about realizing there are none. As Osho said, "Life is not a problem to be solved; it is a mystery to be lived."

Your biggest problem is thinking you should not have them. If you really get it, you see your problems as a gift. If you are in a situation that you feel like you have to solve, take action right now. Do not procrastinate. Do the best you can so you can remove your worries immediately. If you cannot do anything right now, do not let worry take over. It means it is a future situation. There is no way that you can manage future situations because they do not yet exist!

By focusing on your problems, you are training your mind to live in a world of limitations. It is your mind projecting imaginary situations, which creates fear and anxiety. Your emotional problems are not actual problems. You create them with your self-centered thoughts about how you think things should be or how people should behave.

When you dissolve problems, you train your mind to practice radical acceptance. Consequently, you live in a world of infinite possibilities. The quality of your life depends on how you react, not what life throws at you. How would you feel if you lived in a world where there were no problems? What would you create? How would you spend your time? Realize the only problem you have is believing you have one.

LET YOUR SUBCONSCIOUS
WORK FOR YOU

THE WAY YOU LIVE YOUR LIFE, HOW YOU REACT, WHAT YOU believe, and how you experience your day-to-day life is all programmed in your subconscious mind. The subconscious mind works on autopilot. When you are eating, you consciously put food in your mouth, chew it, and then swallow. Once it is inside your belly, your subconscious activates your digestive system. You do not need to do it intentionally. It just happens.

You do not have conscious control over most of the tasks your body needs to do in order to survive. This is why you do not worry that you will stop breathing, that your heart will stop pumping blood, or that your body will stop replacing cells. If you are not doing all of this, who is? That is your subconscious mind. It has an infinite amount of intelligence and organizational capacity. It is the most powerful information processor known in the universe.

For example, if you are driving while thinking about an argument you had with your girlfriend, when your awareness comes back to the present moment, you realize you are three miles farther, you stopped at the red light in time, and you are on the correct way home. So, who was driving the car? That is your subconscious mind. It does not take any vacations. It is always on alert. If the car in front of you stops suddenly, you are going to hit the brakes faster than your conscious mind can process. How can your subconscious mind learn how to drive? How did it know to get you home safely? By repetition! By driving over and over again, your mind created a behavioral program. When your conscious mind stops paying attention, your subconscious programming takes over. Since the subconscious operates without conscious attention, you are unaware that it runs your life. It is time to uninstall what is not working for you.

Think of your mind as a garden; your conscious mind plants seeds into your subconscious. Most of the time, you do not know what you are planting. These are the seeds of your habitual thinking. Scientists have found that people spend 95 percent of the day subconsciously. The conscious mind is in charge for only 5 percent of the day.

Your life is run by your subconscious programming, but did you choose the programs that are running your life? Who installed them? Was it your parents? Was it society? You live your life according to your beliefs, and the sum of all your beliefs creates your conditioning. Your subconscious tapes reproduce your conditioning. Most of your programs were installed when you were a kid. You acquired them by observing your surroundings and installed them without question. Until the age of seven, kids emit theta brain waves. Theta brain waves are responsible for passing information from your conscious to your subconscious mind. Children download incredible amounts of information.

Think about it, how many rules do you need to learn to be a functional member of society? Nature designed a kid to learn.

Kids can process all this information efficiently, so later on, they can survive on their own. Nothing is random in cosmic design. If you learn how to ride a bike as a kid, you remember forever. Adults emit theta brain waves in REM sleep and deep meditation. Your subconscious mind is more susceptible when your brain waves slow down. When you produce melatonin, your brain waves slow down automatically from beta to alpha. This means before you go to sleep and as soon as you wake up are the best times to plant conscious impressions in your subconscious.

When you produce stress hormones, your melatonin levels decrease. When you experience stress, you lose the power to influence your subconscious mind. Sleep is the door to your subconscious. Do not go to sleep with anxiety or feelings of failure. Sleep feeling grateful. Rest in the belief that all your dreams already came true.

One of the first lessons I learned when I began studying yogic philosophy is how the subconscious mind is running my life and how I can rewire it. In Sanskrit, *Chitta* means the subconscious mind. Meditation is planting positive seeds while trimming the roots of fear you carry inside. The psychological imprints left in your subconscious by your daily experiences are called *Samskaras*. In Sanskrit, Samskaras are mental impressions. *Vasanas* are the programs making you react. Vasanas are a dynamic chain of Samskaras. To put it simply, a lot of Samskaras create Vasanas. In scientific terms, a lot of mental impressions create your subconscious programming. Often, when you think you are being spontaneous, you are only repeating the same old reactions. Clear your mind of past impressions. Whatever beliefs and opinions are impressed in your subconscious, you experience. What you program on the inside, you experience on the outside. This is what education actually is. The word educate comes from the Latin root, *educo*, which means develop from within. So, real education means reprogramming your subconscious limitations.

Intelligence is the capacity to respond from moment to moment and not reacting according to a program. You can always reprogram your subconscious. You can always get a new blueprint to run your life. You are spending 95 percent of your day on a program you did not choose. How crazy is this? The subconscious mind works like a cassette recorder. There is no reasoning with it. No one is there; it is just your behavioral tapes reproducing over and over when you lack awareness. You can play any cassette you want, but the cassette recorder cannot compose a song. Your conscious mind is creative, but your subconscious is habitual. Your subconscious plays the behavioral tapes, but it cannot choose between a constructive or a destructive one. The impressions you have installed in your subconscious create the conditions of your reality.

When you want to change something in your life, you usually attempt to change your actions. You constantly struggle to change your actions because you do not understand why you act the way you do. Let's analyze how it actually works: Results come from actions. Actions come from thoughts. Thoughts come from feelings. Feelings come from how you relate to the world. How you relate to the world comes from your subconscious programming.

When you only try to change your actions, you are working so hard to be the best version of your limited self. If you only change your actions instead of your programming, you will be exhausted because you are fighting against your own subconscious mind. How many people focus on a specific diet instead of focusing on eating healthy? Focusing on a diet means only trying to change your actions. Eating healthy is reprogramming your subconscious, which allows you to have a better relationship with food. In one, you are changing your actions. In the other, you are changing your programming.

Carl Jung, the father of modern psychology, said, "Until you make the unconscious conscious, it will direct your life, and you will call it fate." When you change your programming, you relate to the world differently. If you relate to the world differently, you feel and think accordingly. When your feelings and thoughts change, you automatically alter your actions. When you change your actions, results change—without even trying! Your inner programming is the cause, and the circumstances are the effect. It is not the other way around. In other words, your inner world creates your outer world. The biggest obstacle you face to fulfilling all your dreams is exchanging the limited programs your subconscious mind has installed. Change your programs, and everything follows effortlessly. It is really simple. Feelings of deficiency create scarcity, and feelings of sufficiency create abundance. How do you feel?

Being human comes with subconscious default settings. The default settings are a sense of inadequacy, insecurity, and insufficiency. Your programming is limiting the way you experience life. People struggle to take compliments because the compliment is not in accordance with how they perceive themselves. The image of yourself is only an opinion; it is not a fact. You can only accept as much as you think you deserve.

I have a friend who was always struggling to keep his business afloat. When we started working on his consciousness, he said, "I have to be more money-conscious."

I purposefully asked, "What is money conscious?"

He responded, "I need to be firmer on money because every month something happens, and I end up making less."

I told him that he did not have to be money conscious. He needed to be money worthy. He had to expand the way he saw himself to feel worthy of receiving. His subconscious tapes did not allow him to experience abundance. What are you not feeling worthy of receiving? Money? Love? Friendship? Whatever you think you lack is just an outdated program. To remove lack and limitation from your life, you must remove them from your mind first. Be aware because your subconscious only accepts what you feel to be true and not what you think to be true. For example, if you think you should receive more (fill in the blank…), and you do not feel worthy of receiving it, your subconscious will receive the message of not deserving.

Robert Kiyosaki, in his famous book, *Rich Dad, Poor Dad*, explained the difference between the rich and the poor is only subconscious programming. Kiyosaki's "poor dad" was always afraid of taking risks. While his "rich dad" made him work for free because if he gave him a salary, he would always think like an employee. In other words, his poor dad's programming came from lack, while his rich dad came from abundance. Whatever you believe you deserve is what you get.

What do you think you deserve: scarcity or abundance? As

Joseph Murphy said, "Wealth is ultimately nothing more than a subconscious conviction on the part of the individual." The key is to make your subconscious abundant. Never say "I cannot afford it" or "I cannot do it." These statements only close the door of your mind. The universal law is that your subconscious never fails to express the impressions you install. Do not install "I cannot." Instead, install "I can." The moment your subconscious downloads the information, it immediately begins to work on how to manifest it.

Your subconscious is imprinted with nature's intelligence. Nobody taught you how to breathe, digest, or circulate your blood. The subconscious is also the link between your conscious mind and nature's intelligence. Thomas Edison used to take advantage of this knowledge. Whenever he struggled with an invention, he passed the problem to his subconscious. Edison would eventually find the answer in the form of a hunch. He reportedly knew the solution was going to work beforehand. His subconscious always gave him the answer. That is why he said, "Never go to sleep without a request to your subconscious." Edison's persistence was vital to influencing his subconscious mind.

Lack of persistence is one of the main causes of being stuck with the same behavioral tapes. As Napoleon Hill says, "Man has the power to influence his own subconscious mind and, through it, gain the cooperation of infinite intelligence." By persistence and repetition, you can pass voluntary information into your subconscious mind. This is called *autosuggestion*. You can place thoughts, ideas, and desires into your subconscious. Just be careful with the involuntary autosuggestion because your subconscious will reproduce anything you repeat to yourself.

To send an impression to your subconscious, you need to

understand the vehicle to use is your feelings. It cannot be done by positive thinking alone. Feelings are thoughts on steroids. If you see thoughts and feelings working out, thoughts are using the machines with no added weights—and feelings are squatting five hundred pounds. Feeling is the key!

An abundant life begins with a state of mind. Do not let your mindset limit your potential. If you want to pass abundance to your subconscious, feel abundant every day until it is part of your behavioral tapes. After that, you will have the right programming, and your subconscious will work for you! Your subconscious hands over the plan via intuitive signals. When it does, you must act immediately. You will know inside your heart what you need to do. Remember, your destiny is written by you subconsciously.

The subconscious mind does not distinguish between harmful and destructive thoughts or positive and constructive ones. The information passes either way and manifests itself into physical existence. This is why Henry Ford said, "Whether you think you can, or you think you can't—you're right."

Be careful with what you are repeating to yourself. Repetition is critical. Be persistent. Do not program yourself to wake up with negativity. You become what you constantly think of. Your mind is nature's greatest gift. Learn how to use it! Do not take it for granted. Do not accept any destructive tapes. If you learn how to work with the most powerful device you have at your disposal, your life will be an effortless, abundant adventure. So, let your subconscious work for you.

UNDERSTANDING
SURPASSES FORGIVENESS

EACH PERSON IS RAISED IN A UNIQUE WAY. EVERYBODY HAS A different perspective and experiences the world accordingly. For example, Caroline, the editor of this book, has a twin. They were raised by the same parents and went to the same schools, but they see the world completely differently.

First, you were given a name that created your identity. Then, your parents, siblings, and schools taught you how to become a member of society. Usually, people are raised by a punishment and reward system. If you behaved in the way the adults wanted you to, they would tell you are a "good kid" or give you a reward like a piece of candy. If you did not behave as you were "supposed" to, you would get grounded.

People educate children similarly to how they train dogs. This is absurd! The human brain is way more complex than a dog's brain. They taught you how to judge, and you became a master of it. You judge yourself and others without even knowing. This reward versus punishment system was installed in your subconscious, creating the beliefs that you have today. Your conditioning is your internal voice, which judges everything that you do and everything other people do. You base all your judgments according to how you were raised, including religion, political climate, culture, country, social class, and so on. The majority of your programming came from your parents, but where did your parents' programming come from? From their parents! Your parents, just like everyone in this world, are doing the best they can according to how they were raised. So, stop judging! The only way you can get out of this trap is by understanding. Without understanding, you are acting like a dog chasing its own tail.

Your conditioning is always according to the environment. Depending on the environment, you experience the world from a particular perspective. Environment creates conditioning, conditioning creates subconscious programming, and subconscious programming makes you react, behave, and judge everything that happens around you. If your subconscious programming is running your life, you can conclude it is running everyone else's lives too.

The majority of people do not even know their conditioning determines their actions. Knowing this, why do you put so much attention into how other people behave? They are only acting according to how they see the world. There is one earth, but there are billions of worlds. If you were raised given the same name and experience the exact circumstances of the people you are judging, you would act exactly the same. You cannot hold someone accountable for the programs they are not even aware of. If I get angry because your behavior does not fit my models of how you should act, that is my problem for having models in the first place—not yours. Remember, you are experiencing the world based on your conditioning, and your judgment is based on your perception, not necessarily on reality.

Don Miguel Ruiz, a writer of Toltec wisdom, teaches a simple tool to avoid suffering: Do not take anything personally. Everybody is acting according to their models. So why do you think anything is against you? If you take anything personally, you are only defending your conditioning. Nothing that other people do is because of you. It is because of themselves. Even if they insult you, understand that it has nothing to do with you.

Imagine you are listening to your favorite jam while driving. Suddenly, the guy behind you starts honking and screaming. Would you get upset? Only if you take it personally. If you do not, you would still be singing, moving out of the way, or ignoring him. You might even laugh at the paradox that he thinks honking will make him go any faster. You understand this has nothing to do with you. He is driving his car, and you are driving yours. Now, here is when life gets fun. Imagine the same scenario, but earlier, your boss screamed at you because you made a mistake with a client. This time, instead of ignoring him, you take it personally. You get angry and flip him off. Now, you are in a state of reaction. But what changed? What is the difference between both scenarios? The act is the same, but in the second, you took it personally. You even took the fight with your boss personally. When you stop taking things personally, you teach your subconscious that nothing that happens is against you. Whatever your boss said and the guy honking have nothing to do with you. It is just what is happening.

If you take things personally, anybody can steal your most valuable asset: the present moment. When you feel offended, it is your belief system that is getting offended—not you. Why do you need to be right and make other people wrong? Being right is always relative. This type of behavior makes you reactive instead of responsive. When you realize wanting to be right is only defending your conditioning, and your conditioning depends solely on your environment, you stop trying to be right. Making people wrong is a disservice to everyone. If you remain open, you can transcend your conditioning and eliminate all of your defensiveness. As Don Miguel Ruiz said, "Don't take anything personally because by taking things personally, you set yourself up to suffer for nothing." Not taking anything personally allows you to experience the miracle of this moment. Next time you start reacting, remember: Do not judge people—just see the limiting programs they live by.

Your thoughts are not facts; they are merely opinions. So, why do you take them seriously? People usually say that you "need to talk better to yourself." In my opinion, you do not need to talk better to yourself. You need to *listen* better to yourself. If you learn how to listen, you are going to stop reacting and start responding. Reacting is an emotional response that is based on your belief systems. Responding is taking a moment to act accordingly to whatever situation life presents without an emotional response. This is why meditation is so effective. Each time you meditate, you are learning how to listen to your mind.

When you create space between you and your thoughts, you find that you make assumptions about almost everything. When you make assumptions, you believe that whatever you are thinking is true. And just to put it more interesting, you even take them personally. For example, if your girlfriend does not pick up her phone, you make assumptions about why she is not answering. If you call her again, and she still does not answer, you start believing that she is cheating. You were only calling her to say hello, but now you are calling to know who she is with! You begin to take her not answering personally and imagine she is with someone else because you did not bring her flowers on Valentine's Day. The moment she calls you back, she says, "Hey, babe. Sorry, I was talking to my mom." You realize you suffered unnecessarily for nothing. Your mind invented an insane story because you are used to making assumptions. Do yourself a favor and stop it. Stop wasting unnecessary energy with unnecessary worries. Assumptions only exist in your imagination. They are not even real. Assumptions create resistance, and resistance is suffering.

There is an ancient story about a king who wanted to exterminate a small group of people. The wise men went to talk to the king to convince him to spare their lives.

The king said, "If you give me something by tomorrow so that every time I feel sad, I can be happy instead, I will spare your lives."

The following day, the wise men went to see the king and gave him a box.

The king opened it, saw a ring, and started yelling, "I have all the jewelry in the world! Why would I spare your life with this ring?"

The wise men responded, "See what is written inside."

The king looked inside, and the ring said, "This too shall pass." The king acknowledged the lesson and spared their lives. But there is a catch to this story. The king did not realize that when he is happy, this shall pass too! That is why you should not take compliments personally. If someone tells you that you are amazing or tells you that you are horrible, it should not concern you. If you take compliments personally, you start to become addicted to them. You begin pleasing other people so they will keep telling you how great you are. People may change their opinions at any moment; why should you make them important? Whatever they think of you, that is their business and not yours. Opinions have nothing to do with you. It is essential not to take anything personally—good or bad.

In everything you do, the ultimate motive of all your actions is to find joy. And everybody is acting according to their model for how to find it. There is not a person on this planet who acts in opposition to how they perceive the world. The motivation behind every action you do is because you love something, is it not? Yet, sometimes, a loving act manifests in an unloving way. People want to be loved, but they may act in an unloving way to acquire it. For example, my niece loves chocolate, and she loves it so much that sometimes she takes her sister's chocolate. She is not taking it because she is a bad person. She's four years old! The act she is doing may appear unloving, but in reality, it comes from her love of chocolate. So get this, every act is an act of love—always. Your mean boss, the thief on the subway, my beautiful niece, and everyone breathing right now, the core of all actions are always motivated by love.

If you really get this, why would you need to forgive someone? Most importantly, who do you think you are to forgive someone? Understanding surpasses forgiveness. Understanding is the dimension beyond forgiveness. It breaks the cycle of violence. When you feel the need to forgive someone, you are using the same energy as the one who offended you in the first place.

When someone does something unloving to you, do not react with the same energy that caused the problem. Even Einstein acknowledged that we could not solve a problem with the same energy it was created by. Without understanding, you are trying to end violence with more violence or trying to end anger with more anger. Only with understanding can you break the cycle—not with forgiveness.

Forgiveness is trying to fit someone inside your models. When you feel you need to forgive someone, you are taking things personally. When you see a person acting unlovingly ask, "What do you love so much you are willing to hurt others to get it?" By this understanding, you shift your energy from reacting with hate to responding with love and compassion. This does not mean that you accept their behavior. It means you understand. When you do, you do not have the burden of holding any grudges because you know the motivation of their actions always comes from a place of love. When you understand this, you are free.

When you focus on forgiving, you are repressing your emotions. When you try to suppress your emotions, guess what? You think of them even more! Repressed emotions create unloving results. Stop this nonsense of forgiving. Go beyond and seek to understand. Once you do, forgiveness is no longer required. By understanding, compassion arises in your being automatically. Only when you realize that everything you do and have done comes from a place of love can you understand it in others.

Every person uniquely experiences the world. You cannot know how coffee tastes to me. You can only know how it tastes to you, and based on your own taste, you assume how mine tastes. The same applies to everything. When you assume other people's behaviors and beliefs, you tend to judge or empathize based on your perspective. Empathy is putting yourself in other people's shoes. But you do it with your own socks of judgment! You empathize using your conditioning because you bring your beliefs, and with them, you try to imagine what the other is feeling. Being empathetic is like trying to know how my coffee tastes. In other words, a complete waste of time. As the song by Kings of Leon says, "I walk a mile in your shoes, and now I'm a mile away—and I got your shoes!"

Empathy is not compassion. True compassion is understanding that if you lived and experienced the same circumstances as someone else, you would act, think, and behave in the same manner as the people you are judging. When you empathize, you automatically see through a lens of pettiness because you think you know better than them. There is a difference between compassion and pity. Pity is violent and judgmental. True compassion is understanding, which means there is no form of judgment.

How you judge others is a reflection of how you judge yourself. Whatever you tend to judge in others gives an insight into where you have a limited perspective. It is only revealing where you are not free. Whenever someone or something triggers you, that is your opportunity for growth. The more limited view you have of yourself, the more you react to what other people do.

Now that you know everybody is doing the best they can— based on their programming and that every act is an act of love— this also includes *you*. Stop judging what you did in the past. You were trying your best with the awareness you had at the time. Learn your lesson and move on. Understand that everything you have ever done and will ever do comes from a place of love.

Increase your awareness, so your acts of love do not produce unloving results. All you need to do is just *be who you are.* Remove whatever is blocking you from experiencing and expressing love in every aspect of your life. We are only reflections of each other. True compassion is polishing your own mirror. You work on yourself so much that your life is a reflection of love itself. Your mirror is so clear that everyone else can release their suffering just by being around you. Be the environment of love. Working on yourself is the most you can do for humanity. Working on yourself is true compassion.

FREE YOURSELF FROM THE ILLUSION THAT YOU ARE NOT ENOUGH

YOU TEND TO REACT TO SITUATIONS WITHOUT UNDERSTANDING why. When something goes wrong, your subconscious programming reacts automatically and predictably. If someone or something gets you upset enough to change your internal state, you usually react compulsively instead of responding accordingly. This situation is the perfect opportunity for self-evaluation. If you do not get stuck in the reactive stage, you can obtain valuable information by observing what is triggering you.

The question is, are you aware enough to use your triggers as instruments of growth—or are you too busy being angry? Triggers are channels for self-discovery. Life will always present you with the perfect conditions to reveal where you are not free. A trigger is just a limited belief traveling from your subconscious into your conscious mind, which allows you to trace it, understand it, and transcend it. For example, if you are insecure about your weight and someone asks, "Are you on a diet?" Your limited belief makes you have an internal reaction, and your whole state changes immediately. This may ruin your entire day, but it has nothing to do with the question. What it is truly revealing is that you are not comfortable with your body and feel you need to look a certain way to be loved.

You have two options. You can get offended and blame the other person—or you can use the situation to see where you have a limited belief. A limited belief is a false perception that makes you feel like you are not enough, and it is not allowing you to enjoy this moment fully. Think about it, what if they asked the same question to Lebron James? Would he react and get upset? Obviously not! It is not about what happens to you. It is about how you react. No one can give you happiness or unhappiness; they can only reflect your inner being. If you cannot sit with a person or situation, it is the perfect opportunity to become a more powerful human being. Every challenge is an opportunity to learn and wake up. Every adversity comes by a counterpart advantage.

Socrates was married to Xanthippe. She was a nagging and mean wife, but he said that being married to her was an excellent way to practice philosophy. He said, "By all means, marry. If you get a good wife, you'll become happy; if you get a bad one, you'll become a philosopher."

Whenever a relationship, friendship, job, or whatever you are dealing with brings out the madness in you, be glad. All that is happening is that what was unconscious is being brought to the surface. Instead of reacting and being caught in the emotional response, take a step back and ask some questions: What limited belief do I have inside myself that is making me react? What model am I carrying that is not allowing me to be in this situation? How am I allowing the opinion of others to determine how I choose to live?

If somebody did or said something and you get upset, that is your problem. It has nothing to do with the person or the situation. The trigger was already inside you. When you live according to someone else's expectations, you are trying to mold yourself into someone's limitations. When someone triggers you, say (probably inside your head), "Thank you for showing me where I am not free, where I am still clinging to a model of how I believe the universe should be."

Self-mastery comes when you are absolutely responsible for everything that happens to you. If you look closely, you can begin noticing the pattern of your conditional responses. You only act defensively because your beliefs are getting attacked. One key lesson that I learned is that I am responsible for finding my own happiness. I know that when I do not experience what I want, I am often blocking it. Instead of focusing on outside circumstances, I work on my inner awareness to see what limited belief blocks my energy. A happy or unhappy life is my creation. This means that I always take responsibility for my responses. Being responsible means not blaming others for your unhappiness. When you do this, you shift your consciousness from blaming someone who upsets you to being responsible for your relationship to life. There is nothing wrong with the world. You can make it heaven or hell, according to your approach.

When you start taking responsibility for every situation you experience, you realize that life is happening *for* you—not *to* you. Every uncomfortable situation you encounter, life is working in your favor to free you from your current limitations. Life presents the same lesson over and over again until you learn it.

One common subconscious limitation is the belief that you are not enough. Let's analyze what happens in an abusive relationship. People tend to blame their partners instead of looking at their self-abuse. The relationship you have with yourself is a reflection of the relationship you have with others. Any abusive relationship is because you accept it. The limit of your self-abuse is the limit you tolerate from others. Please understand that no one abuses you more than you abuse yourself. This needs to stop.

How long are you going to wait until you realize your worth? As Buddha said, "If your compassion does not include yourself, it is incomplete." Life will always present you with the right people to reveal where you need to grow. Your abusive relationship is the vehicle in which life is trying to teach you that you are enough. Life wants you to realize that the core of your being is love. Life wants you to express all your creativity and joy. It is trying to free you from your sense of inadequacy via a limited individual who is doing the best they can with their own level of awareness. If a situation, relationship, or whatever you are experiencing did not go the way you want it to, realize that life is setting you up for success. Every situation that happens in your life is a gift. In each experience, there is always a hidden treasure. Free yourself from the illusion that you are not enough.

Until you become aware of your behavior, you will constantly repeat the same patterns. Whatever gets you upset is your biggest blessing. Life creates situations that shake you and make you react to remove what is blocked inside of you. Your triggers are the access to your freedom. If you do not like someone, it is because they are reflecting something you do not like about yourself. Rather than judging them, embrace them. They are the part of you that needs to grow.

You usually try to solve your problems by protecting yourself. You believe the problems you face are a threat, and you react in fear. Real transformation comes when you see your triggers as they are meant to be: instruments for growth. You experience your limitations to get free of them. You are always looking for peace, but where is it? This has a very simple answer. You look for peace in the absence of it. You look for peace where you are not feeling peaceful. You look for harmony whenever you feel disharmonious. Do not get busy complaining about the person or situation that is making you lose your peace. Better, use it to explore your inner world. In what situations do you feel conflict? This is where your work begins. Whatever existence gives you, find a way to use it for your benefit because it is tailor-made for you.

Growth always takes place outside your comfort zone. You tend to see adversity as something terrible. You cling to what you like, and you avoid what you do not. You believe you should escape adversity. This is why it is hard to get out of your comfort zone. Let me reframe what adversity really is: Adversity is your *privilege*.

If you think about it, you do not deal with that much adversity in your life. Whenever it presents itself, be grateful for it. It comes with so many possibilities for growth. As Seneca, a Stoic philosopher, said, "No man is more unhappy than he who never faces adversity. For he is not permitted to prove himself."

You were made to believe that all of your problems will go away when you make a certain amount of money or enter the perfect relationship. Why would you like a life without adversity? Is a life without challenges worth living? Isn't overcoming adversity one of the most enjoyable things in life?

The most inspiring people are those who overcome adversity. Like an Olympian athlete who got injured and returned to win the gold medal. Or someone born in a violent neighborhood and became a good businessman or author. Overcoming adversity is one of the most enjoyable experiences you can have. It makes life worth living. Invite adversity into your life. Look at it as the blessing that it really is. You should feel privileged that you have passed through so many challenges to be ready for the one you are being presented now. How do you know this is the experience you need? Because it is the one you are having! You are ready to face this challenge. I am not saying it is easy, but I am saying you should enjoy it. That is your privilege.

THE DOORWAY TO
YOUR INTELLIGENCE
IS YOUR HEART

HAVE YOU EVER ASKED YOURSELF WHO IS THE VOICE TALKING inside your head? *Why is it judging everything around me? Does it ever shut up? If it's the one who's talking, am I the one who's listening?* You are not the voice in your head. You are the one who notices it. You are the witness of your life.

When you get caught up in your thoughts, you identify with them and believe they are real. Thoughts exist separately from you. Understanding that you are not your thoughts is fundamental for your growth. This realization is the first step to taking control of your life.

Ramana Maharshi was an Indian *jivanmukta*. In Vedanta philosophy, *jivan* means one who lives, and *mukta* means liberated. A jivanmukta is a liberated being who lives in the world for the sake of humanity without any personal attachments. When Ramana Maharshi was sixteen, he had a near-death experience. Instead of fighting death, he surrendered to it. He experienced the death of his physical body, but his awareness was still there. He ended up surviving, but he no longer identified himself with his body or his thoughts. He attained a state of liberation, which people called *Buddha-nature* or *Christ consciousness*. People from all over the world started attending his spiritual teachings. He would explain how to obtain liberation, nirvana, or jivanmukta by a method of negation. In other words, acknowledging *who you are not* to discover *who you really are.*

Whatever you can see, you are not it. The very act of perceiving shows that you are not what you perceive. What you perceive is constantly changing, but does the perceiver change? The body you had as a kid is different than the body you have now. The body changed, but your awareness never did. This is what yogis call *witness consciousness* or your *true self.* How can you know you are not the person in front of you? Because you can see them. So, by definition, whatever you can perceive is not you. You are not your body because you can see it. You can see your legs, arms, stomach, hair, and so on. Additionally, you are not your organs because you can perceive them. You are not your lungs, liver, heart, brain, joints, and so on. After that, go into your thoughts. Start observing them and notice how they pass like clouds in the sky. Once you create a separation between you and your thoughts, you realize you are not them. This is where the fun begins because you realize that the thought of not being a thought is a thought itself. The only way you can experience reality as it really is is to transcend thought. When you identify yourself with your thoughts, you think you are the clouds, limited. In reality, you are the sky, infinite. When you are in an airplane and look through the window, you watch the clouds go by. It can be sunny or rainy, but you are above it all, watching it happen. This is the difference between *being* and *thinking.* In being, you are your true self. In thinking, you identify yourself with thought, which is limited by your perception. You can observe your thoughts, but who is the one who is watching? That's you! You are the awareness behind them. Who are you? There is no intellectual answer. You are the answer!

I remember when I realized that I am not the voice in my head. I used to do yoga at a studio in Los Angeles called Tantris. At the beginning of each class, we chanted, *Lokah Samastah Sukhino Bhavantu,* which means: "May all beings everywhere be happy and free, and may the thoughts, words, and actions of my own life contribute in some way to the happiness and freedom for all." I was fascinated by the part of the mantra that said, "my thoughts ... contribute to the happiness and freedom for all." I was raised to believe that if I do good things, good things happen. However, this mantra is saying that even my thoughts have to be peaceful. So, my thoughts are not me? Can I actually control my thoughts? If I am not my thoughts, who am I? All these questions started to appear in my life. Suddenly, I realized that if I can observe my thoughts, I am not them! This simple mantra planted a seed in my rational mind and created the first separation between me and my thoughts. This realization is the beginning of freedom.

When you stop believing you are your thoughts, you can begin observing them. The moment you transcend thought, a higher level of consciousness becomes automatically activated. You start living more by intuition and less by rationality. Scientists have found that rational decisions are made by the *neocortex*, and intuitive decisions are made from the *limbic system*. Your rationality is limited because it only repeats and reacts to what it knows, but your intuition is unlimited because you are in tune with the unknown. Thought is nothing but the accumulation of the past. You cannot think of the unknown. You can only project what you know. Have you ever had a hunch so strong that you did not understand why, but you needed to act upon it? You cannot rationalize it, but you feel the need to do it. Many times, your rational mind convinces you not to listen to your intuition. Your fears and insecurities take over and convince you with excuses: "This is not the right time," "I am not good enough," or "What would people think?" Intuition is always in alignment with your dharma. Your dharma is your inner wisdom guiding you. The more space you create between you and your thoughts, the more intuitive decisions you will make. Clear your mental disturbances and live in tune with your inner guidance.

Why do you believe that you are your thoughts? Because you are too close to them! If you see what happens when you are angry, sad, or emotionally suffering, there is no space between you and the thoughts creating these emotions. You suffer from your depressions and anxieties because you identify with them. Instead of saying, "I am depressed," say, "I am experiencing depression." You are not your depression. Depression only exists in your mind—not in reality. You give power to your depression by identifying with it. As spiritual teacher Tony de Mello says, "Before enlightenment, I used to be depressed; after enlightenment, I continue to be depressed." What he means is that he does not identify himself with his depression anymore. There is depression—and there is him.

Zen master Suzuki said, "Enlightenment is like everyday consciousness, but two inches above the ground." These two inches are the space between the witness and the witnessed.

There is a story about a disciple who approached a Zen master and said, "Master, I have no peace of mind. Please bring peace to my mind."

The master responded, "Bring out your mind, and I will pacify it."

The disciple replied, "I cannot bring it to you because I cannot find it."

The master responded, "There I pacify your mind."

The disciple was enlightened after this insight because he realized that the mind is an illusion. Never forget that you are not your thoughts—you are the witness of them.

There is a difference between acting and reacting. Reacting makes you a slave to external circumstances. Acting makes you a master of your own life. When you are in a state of reaction, you believe you are your thoughts. Reaction comes from unawareness, while action comes from awareness. When you experience any emotional suffering, just watch your behavior and create space between you and your feelings. Do not try to find a solution. Observe the distance between you and whatever is making you suffer. The moment you start creating space, their power automatically dissolves. It is not about denying these types of emotions. It is about letting them pass through you.

If you suppress anger, sadness, or emotional suffering, you will overcompensate in other aspects of your life. Allowing your feelings eliminates the possibility of suffering. The uncontrolled mind behaves like an enemy. It reacts. Learn how to use your mind; if not, it will use you.

Descartes said, "I think; therefore, I am." People have accepted this phrase as gospel and believe that they are their thoughts. If you think, therefore you are, who are you when you are asleep?

Who are you when you are not thinking? Who are you when you are sedated? Did you stop existing? Of course not! Please understand that you *are*; therefore, you think.

Thinking is a power you have. It allows you to plan, remember, fantasize, and so on, but it is not who you are. Thinking is only a tiny aspect of your being. As Maharishi Mahesh Yogi said, "It is childish and ridiculous to base one's life on the level of thinking." Thinking without awareness is like driving a car without a driver. Without you, the mind cannot do anything. The state of being is the most beautiful way to live life. When you are in love, you do not think you are in love. You are being love. You are not your mind; you are the master of it.

Let's go a step further and analyze what a thought is. A thought always comes from the past. It always comes from the known. By identifying yourself with your thoughts, you are living in the past. Awareness returns you to the present. When you lack awareness, you live in the past, reacting predictably according to your subconscious programming. So, if you think, therefore you are, by definition, you are not! Because you are not here, you are always in the past. The more you think, the less you are.

Thinking is the foundation of doing, but what is the foundation of thinking? In order to think, you need to be. Thought comes from your intellect. Your intellect is the best employee you could ever hire, but it is the worst boss you can work for. It is a servant and not a master. This is the difference between knowledge and wisdom.

Knowledge comes from the intellect, from accumulation of past information, and wisdom comes from the heart, from silence, and from quieting your mind so you can access the full intelligence of your consciousness. Knowledge comes from the outside. Wisdom comes from inside. As Mooji said, "Attempting to understand consciousness with your mind is like trying to illuminate the sun with a candle."

The only thing you need to change is the order in which you trust your mind. First, trust your intuition, and second, trust your rationality. As Nicola Tesla said, "Instinct is something which transcends knowledge." Meditation opens the door to intuition because it separates you from your thinking. The intellect always looks for what it can *get*. The heart always looks for what it can *give*. Do not work for your rationality. Let it work for you. Do not let your heart follow your intellect. Let your intellect follow your heart.

How many times has your mind taken a small piece of uncertain information to create a story, and it ended up consuming you? Identification with the mind causes thoughts to be compulsive. Let's suppose you are taking a walk in the park and suddenly see a dog—the same breed of dog that your ex-girlfriend used to have. Instantly, your mind starts creating thoughts about your relationship, the breakup, the good times you shared, and how you may still be together if you had done something different. Your emotional state changes completely just because you saw a dog!

Thought is always rooted in the past. Your mind tends to deceive you. Every judgment you have is a story your mind is making up. Just because you think about it does not mean it is true. Thoughts are remarkable instruments of deception. They can make you believe anything. Investigate your thoughts. If you put question marks at the end of your concerns, you will see that there are never truths. They are always just opinions. As Shakespeare said, "There is nothing good or bad, but thinking makes it so." When an undesirable thought gets your attention, replace it with an uplifting one right away. Either you control your mind—or your mind controls you. Do not believe when you think you are unworthy. Do not believe when you feel you are not good enough. Do not believe when you think you are not beautiful. Do not believe in the mental boundaries you create. Do not believe everything you think!

Your mind behaves like water. Water assumes the shape of its container, and your mind assumes the shape of your thoughts. Your mind develops the qualities you pour into it. Do you know what you are feeding your mind? Be aware of the toxic waste you put into it. You fill it with worries, anxieties, expectations, and fears—and then complain that you are stressed. You are constantly receiving information from social media, Netflix, the news, etc. Social media can be an excellent tool—but be careful how you use it. The content you are exposing your mind to ultimately shapes your thoughts. Remember, pain that has not yet come is avoidable.

There is a story about a Chinese farmer who found a horse.

His neighbor exclaimed, "You are so lucky!"

He calmly responded, "You never know."

The next day, the farmer's son broke his leg riding the horse.

His neighbor said, "You are so unlucky."

The farmer responded, "You never know."

The next day, the king came to recruit all the young men for war. They did not draft his son because he had a broken leg.

The neighbor came and said, "You are so lucky."

The farmer responded, "You never know."

The whole process of life has immense complexity, and your rational mind cannot understand the entire purpose of any situation. Usually, when you attempt to make a sound decision, you consider all the data you have. However, if you really think about it, you can consider an infinite amount of data for any decision you make. This is why making decisions creates stress. The more you are in tune with your intuitive mind, the less stress you experience making any decision because the intelligence of your full consciousness is guiding you.

The beauty of life is that you cannot rationalize it. If you could, what would be the point of being here? Stop thinking about your life and start living it. Think less and feel more. Nothing can satisfy the mind. It always wants more and more and more. So, stop being so much of a thinker and start being more of a lover because the doorway to your intelligence is your heart. Listen to it!

IT IS NOT A MATTER
OF HOPE—IT IS ONLY A
MATTER OF TIME

IF YOU START TO NOTICE YOUR THOUGHT PATTERNS, YOU WILL FIND that most of the time, your focus is on what you are trying to avoid and not what you want to create. Wherever attention goes, it grows. The secret of creation is attention. So, what are you focusing on? Life will give you anything you ask for. In fact, it has already given you everything you asked for.

The more you try to avoid something, the more attention you give it. Why think of something if you do not want it? This dimension is wonderful. You are here to experience whoever you believe yourself to be. Life will present people and circumstances that match the concept you have of yourself. The first step to changing anything is to acknowledge that what you are experiencing now you have created. Acceptance shifts attention from blame to beneficiary consciousness (more on this later!) When you want to change something without accepting the way things are, you create resistance. If you want to have a different experience, do not do it from a place where you believe what you did was wrong. Do it because what you are experiencing is not an accurate statement of who you are right now.

You probably know someone who is always focusing on the worst possible outcome, and paradoxically, even when something goes their way, they are still afraid that they will run out of luck. When you try to avoid something, it is usually because you are attempting to prevent experiencing a negative feeling in the future. But where is the future? What you are trying to avoid you are experiencing now! Fear and judgment are two powerful methods of creation. They draw the experience to you like a magnet. Think about it, whenever you are afraid or judgmental, what are you really doing? You are putting all of your attention on what you are trying to avoid. No wonder that you experience so many things you do not want to. Things are kept alive by attention, and they die by indifference. If you try to avoid anything with great effort, you will fall into it without effort.

Everything you do is a statement of who you are. When your actions are not in alignment with the concept you have of yourself, you experience scarcity. You get exhausted because your attention is all over the place. You are thinking one thing, feeling another, and acting totally different. It is like taking an Uber and constantly changing the directions to where you want to go. It would be total luck if you ever arrive at your destination. Your focus is in so many directions. You are trying to avoid the highway by your fears and insecurities. But guess what? It is a holiday. There is no traffic. Every day is a holiday where you can create whatever you choose. Traffic only exists in the mind. Focus on what you want—and do not take your attention away until you experience it. By focusing on it, you are giving the driver of your subconscious mind the correct destination. Your most incredible power is your capacity to choose. What are you choosing to experience? If you do not like it, choose again! An abundant life begins with a state of mind.

Adults perceive a world of constraints and limitations, but kids do not even know this experience exists. They live in a world of limitless possibilities.

One day, my five-year-old niece said, "Daddy, I want a big toy house so I can climb it!"

My brother replied, "Sweetie, we need a house with a big garden so it will fit."

She asked, "Okay, why don't you buy a big house?"

My brother responded, "Because you need a lot of money to buy a house with a garden."

She said, "So, why don't you order money through Amazon? When it comes, we can buy it so I can climb my toy house."

When you focus on what you want, you shift your attention from constraints to possibilities. Your job is not to know how this is going to happen. It is only to open the door in your mind. You do not need to have all the answers for how your creative desires will come to life. This is why Jesus said, "Become like children to enter the kingdom of heaven." If your attention is on gratitude, abundance, and peace, guess what you will end up experiencing? Your universe is going to be harmonious like heaven on earth. What you are experiencing now is the result of inattention. What you *will* experience is the result of attention.

Everything that exists in the world began in the form of a thought. Thoughts create energy, and energy creates matter. You are a creator, and you design your life every minute. The tools of creation are thoughts, feelings, words, and actions. Everything begins and ends in your mind. The most powerful thoughts are always the ones that contain joy and gratitude. Your only job is to expand the concept of who you are and allow life to present you with the perfect conditions. Your body is the perfect example of nature's intelligence organizing everything in perfect sync. You have about thirty-seven trillion cells, and they all have to know what the other cells are doing simultaneously. A single cell has to do about six trillion things per second. Even if just one cell does not do its job, it creates problems for the whole system. Not even the most advanced computer can organize this amount of information. So, to think your rational mind has all the answers is like trying to read blindfolded in a language you do not even speak! The universe has infinite organizational capacity, and if you send the right signals, it will align everything for you.

You think around seventy thousand thoughts a day, so how can you be aware of all of them? You do not have to! You have an internal system that tells you what types of thoughts you are thinking. It is called *emotion*. Emotion literally means energy in motion. Emotions represent an amplified thought pattern. Feelings are the language of your cells. Your emotions are letting you know if you are acting from a place of fear or love. When you feel anxious, afraid, and insecure, your emotional guidance tells you that your focus is on something you are trying to avoid. Conversely, if you feel excited, creative, and optimistic, your emotional compass says that you are putting the cosmic computer and all its organizational power to work for you. Thoughts attract other thoughts. It works like a snowball rolling down a mountain; the initial ball is small, but it becomes larger and larger as it starts to move downhill. Eventually, the little snowball that started at the top of the mountain is a gigantic, formidable avalanche. But be careful because it works with negative thoughts too. One can attract another, and before you know it, you have a whole mountain of negativity. If you do not want it, why think about it? What is the point of focusing on the wrong things?

On the surface of your mind, you get an idea. With one positive thought mixed with the right feeling, you start attracting another—and then another—each one with less effort and more power until it accesses a deeper part of your brain, your subconscious mind. A feeling of excitement is a sign that you are in tune with nature's intelligence.

The better you feel, the more you are in alignment with the version of yourself you want to experience. If you are not excited about it, then it is not your path. Do not spend time justifying not feeling good. Do not do anything out of a sense of obligation. Do it out of a sense of opportunity to express who you are. Obligation looks like fear, and opportunity looks like joy.

Whatever you do, have a feeling of gratitude and not a feeling of "I have to do it." As Esther Hicks said, "You did not come into this environment to create through action. Instead, your action is meant to be a way in which you enjoy what you have created through thought."

Action is not meant to create your inner experience. Action is intended to reflect your inner being. Set your mind to whatever you want to experience, and the right action will happen automatically. Beyond the perception of limitation is the world of possibilities. Beyond the perception of scarcity is the abundant universe.

As long as you believe someone else is responsible for your experience, you forget your power. Mastery is when you are completely responsible for what happens to you because you renounce the belief that the outside world has power over you. Remember, there are no victims; there are only creators. The person who thinks, talks, and expects wealth, prosperity, joy, freedom, and fun attracts or is attracted to them. Mastering your internal emotional compass is essential to experiencing the broadest version of yourself. When you ask for something as if you do not have it already, the request itself is an energetic statement of lack.

If you focus on wanting instead of already having it, you will experience the wanting itself because that is the energetic signal you emit. The correct energetic statement is one of gratitude and appreciation. You cannot say thank you for something you have not received yet. When you are grateful before receiving it, life has no choice but to give it to you. Instead of saying, "I want money," say, "Thank you for all the money that is flowing through my life."

Do not use people and situations to give you what you want to experience. Instead, realize you are the creator and *use* life situations to express what you *already* are. Remember, the reason you are in this physical dimension is to experience the highest thought you have about yourself. Please understand that you already are what you want to become. Think like it, dream like it, act like it, eat like it, be it, and believe it! And realize it is not a matter of hope; it is only a matter of time.

EFFORTLESS REFLECTION
OF MY OWN FREQUENCY

Have you ever been attracted to someone who is not exactly your type, but for some reason, you are intrigued by their presence? Have you ever entered a room and felt calm and peaceful? Conversely, have you met someone you do not like being around—not because they did something to you but because something you cannot explain pulls you apart from that person? Have you ever entered a space where you feel weird as soon as you walked in. When you asked yourself why, you could not find a rational explanation?

When you go to a beach town like Puerto Escondido in Oaxaca, everybody seems to have a chill vibe. People are surfing, gazing at the sunset, and lying on the sand. The minute you get there, you feel a sense of peace. On the other hand, when you travel to New York City, the energy is more frenetic. You find yourself keeping up with the locals, rushing to meet the subway, or arriving at one destination—yet already thinking about the next one. Your body and mind seem to act accordingly to the environment you are in.

Your body is like a magnet. It has a vibrational field that emits and receives electromagnetic energy. You are constantly emitting information based on your intentions and feelings. Your vibrational field works as an interplay between the energy you emit and the energy you receive. Think of this energy as an exchange of information. The information you are sending is the outcome you end up experiencing. When you grab two magnets and place them facing each other, they stick together with a force if the electromagnetic field is aligned. Even if you do not want them to come together, you will not be able to stop them from colliding. If the magnets do not complement each other, even if you superglue them, they will repel. Whatever you encounter in your life is just a vibrational match of the signal you are emitting.

The universe works in a dynamic trade-off. Everything is always vibrating. You are sending and receiving information all the time. Giving and receiving is the natural flow of existence. Some people have trouble giving, and some have trouble receiving. I have a friend who gives love to everyone he meets. His intentions are pure and innocent, but he does not know how to receive love. Energetically, he is interfering with the flow of the universe. Giving and receiving is the exact exchange on the other side of the coin. If you block any part of this energetic flow, it will create a clot, like your body creates when you stop circulating blood. This includes relationships, money, work, and everything in your existence. When you tune in your cosmic radio, you get better reception. To take control of your vibrations, you need to take responsibility for your inner state.

Everything in the universe is energy. Energy vibrates in different patterns and produces different densities. Thoughts, feelings, and words are subtle forms of energy. The denser the energy, the more you can perceive it. For example, a thought comes to your mind, and if the energy emits a strong enough signal, it produces a feeling. A feeling has a denser vibration than a thought. The densest form of energy is matter. If you understand the power of your vibrational field, you can use it to your advantage. How can you control the information you are emitting?

Feelings are the language of how your cells exchange information. The key to radiating a high vibration is feeling. This is why positive thinking is ineffective. You can think positively all you want, but if you do not have an elevated emotion, your vibrational field will never expand. An elevated emotion is an uplifting one like joy, bliss, gratitude, freedom, and appreciation. Similarly, a downgraded emotion is shame, guilt, fear, and victimization. You cannot have the life you want by trying to fix the life you do not want. It is not vibrationally liable. You are swimming against the current and getting exhausted in the process. You are emitting a signal and trying to superglue whatever you accidentally invite. Until you change your vibration, you will always recycle your experiences. Instead of fixing the life you do not want, why not focus on creating the one you do? Why not start expanding your vibrational field and begin attracting people and circumstances on your new vibrational rate? Do not try to fix the life you do not want. Create the one you do.

People confuse the vibration of *wanting* with the vibration of *having*. The energy of wanting sends the signal of yearning. Focusing on wanting creates anxiety because you emit a vibration of not having it in the first place. Focusing on having creates excitement because you emit a vibration of gratitude. In other words, wanting produces lack, and having produces abundance.

If there is something you wish to experience, do not *want* it—*choose* it! Realize you are the source. The quickest way to change your vibration from wanting to having is simple: Whatever you wish to experience, give it to others, and you immediately shift your energy. Remember that the universe works dynamically, and giving and receiving are interrelated. For example, if you want to experience love, patience, or wealth, find someone to give it to, and you will realize you already have it in the first place. The universe's abundance is beyond measure. There are more stars in the sky than you can ever dream of. There are between forty million and one billion sperm in every single ejaculation, but only one is needed to create human life. It is your birthright to have an abundant life. The only thing you need to remember is you are the source of your own abundance.

Scientists found that alpha brain waves are responsible for a state of calmness, relaxation, and higher forms of creativity. In yogic terms, alpha brain waves are *Sattvic*. Sattva is the equanimity of the mind. So, how can you produce alpha brain waves? Studies have shown that holding grudges suppresses alpha brain waves. Resentment suppresses the equanimity of the mind. When you are suppressing alpha brain waves, you are depressing your ability to create. Forgiveness is essential to be in equilibrium, but remember understanding surpasses forgiveness! Life is really fair. If you take the poison of anger, you are the one who is going to get intoxicated—and not the one who made you angry.

Elevated emotions create faster vibrational waves, and downgraded emotions create slower ones. Think about elevated emotion as a Ferrari versus a downgraded one like a bicycle. With this in mind, I would like to introduce a scientific experiment called the Maharishi effect. This phenomenon studied how vibration changes when people are doing a meditation technique called Transcendental Meditation (TM). TM changes the vibrational rate of the meditator, which affects the vibrational rate of an entire area.

Gregg Braden explains, during the Israeli-Lebanese war in the early 1980s, advanced TM meditators were asked to meditate in the conflict area. During this window of time, terrorist incidents, crime, emergency room visits, and traffic accidents all declined in number. When the participants stopped, the statistics reversed. Higher vibrations created by uplifting emotions travel faster than downgraded ones. The Maharishi effect shows the number of people needed to affect the vibration in an area is just the square root of 1 percent of the population. In other words, a Ferrari vibration beats a lot of bicycles. When you change your vibrational rate, you change the entire energy field of your surroundings. Also, this scientific experiment demonstrates that it is faster to create the life you want than to live a life you don't. Just for the record, this is the type of meditation that I do, and it changed my vibrational rate faster than a tornado.

One of the *48 Laws of Power* by Robert Greene is "Be royal in your fashion, act like a king to be treated like one." He explains this law in a psychological manner, but I would like to explore the vibrational aspect of it. If you are already being what you are trying to become, people and circumstances will respond to your vibration. Remember the energy of having versus wanting. You need to live as if your prayers have already been answered.

The material world—everything you can perceive with your five senses—is the slowest form of vibration. If you are being, thinking, behaving, talking, and dreaming as your higher self, it is just a matter of time until you experience it in the material world. One shortcut you can use to emit a high vibration is gratitude. A thankful heart is always in alignment with the abundance of the universe. Gratitude makes use of nature's intelligence in your favor. When you are grateful, it means you emit the energy of having—and life has no choice but to give it to you.

Karma is not a punishment and reward system. In Sanskrit, the word *Karma* simply means action. When you say that something happened because of your Karma, you are only saying that it is your own doing. In other words, everything that comes to you is a return of what comes out from you. Your thoughts, feelings, and actions leave behind a certain pattern of information. The information (or vibration) you leave behind corresponds with what you will experience later. Karma is a vibrational exchange. As Nikola Tesla said, "If you want to find the secrets of the universe, think in terms of energy, frequency, and vibration."

To access your full intelligence, you need to control your energy. Usually, thinking goes in one direction, feeling goes in another, and action goes in another. The vibration emitted is a mess, which brings confusion. And confusion brings suffering. This is why you put so much effort but do not get optimal results. Full intelligence is always in alignment. If you align your thinking, feeling, and action, you create clarity—and clarity brings bliss.

Remember that your intellect is limited. Do not make it about your intellect. Make it about your vibration. Be aware of the frequency you are emitting. There is a difference between linear and vertical growth. Linear depends on circumstances.

Vertical depends on vibrations. Linear is continuously oscillating between pain and pleasure. Vertical is always stable in the bliss of your existence. Focus on your vertical growth. Start living by this mantra: Effortless reflection of my own frequency.

DISCIPLINE BRINGS
YOU FREEDOM

NOWADAYS, THE WORD *DISCIPLINE* HAS A BAD REPUTATION. YOU think of discipline as a process you have to do, a task you will not enjoy, or something you have to endure to get somewhere else. You see discipline as strictness, control, or something that is being imposed on you. Your habits are just programs running by your subconscious. To replace an outdated program or habit, you need the discipline to make a software update.

It is natural that any organism fights for its own survival— so the old programs will fight to remain alive. They create resistance to stay in your subconscious. This is where you need to be persistent until the new software is fully installed and the old becomes obsolete. You can exchange what you enjoy, what you call fun, and even what you like to eat. I am the living proof that this is totally true. Years ago, I started experimenting with different types of fasting. I realized that drinking coffee did not create an insulin spike, so I could drink it and remain in a fasted state. The problem was that I liked to drink coffee with milk. The milk created an insulin spike, so it messed up the whole process. I had three options: stop fasting and miss all of the potential benefits, stop drinking coffee, or change the way I drink it. So, I decided I was only going to drink black coffee. It did not take long until I started enjoying it. Once the new program was installed, when I tried coffee with milk, even to this day, it tastes horrible! I discovered something more profound than how I drink coffee. I found that if I can have the discipline to update the old program, I can literally create the life, body, and relationships I want without putting in any effort later.

What is the need for discipline? Discipline is simply acquiring skill. It is updating your software. Discipline is a way of expression. If you want to express something inside yourself, you have to develop the necessary skill. For example, let's say you have a musical mind. Unless you know how to play the instrument of your liking and acquire a basic skill level, it is going to be impossible for you to express whatever you have in mind. As you develop your skill further, your level of expression increases, and your creativity rises. Therefore, your life becomes more enjoyable. Whatever you do in life, you need to acquire the skills to express it and fully enjoy it.

There is no possibility of pleasure without skill. It is like trying to enjoy a forty-year-old bottle of wine. Without developing a sensitive palate, it tastes the same as a cheap one. Developing new skills allows you to enjoy all that this world has to offer. The great pleasures and joys in life come in the form of learning a skill. Learning a skill is not an unpleasant task. On the contrary, if you think about it, you have more fun when you can express something you learn.

There is a concept in Zen Buddhism called *Shoshin*, which means beginner's mind. When you are new to something and do not know anything about it, you have to develop a unique mindset to acquire the knowledge or skill you want to obtain. Your mind needs to be empty to learn something new. If it is not, it only repeats the same mechanical, habitual actions. If you want to learn how to surf, when you take your first lessons, you will be totally engaged in the process. The unfamiliar situation you are in will make you notice how the surfboard feels, how the waves are, and how your body balances when you are standing on the board. You will not be thinking of what you want for lunch or what you have to do tomorrow. You are going to be fully present. And the moment you can ride your first wave, you will feel an inexplicable, joyful sensation.

Why not apply this type of mindset in everything you do? A beginner's mindset is free of preconceptions because you do not bring any baggage to the learning process. You are open and free from expectations because you are full of curiosity. Your attention is 100 percent in the activity you are doing because there is no room for distraction. You are exploring instead of searching. There is immense pleasure in learning, and it is essential for your evolution. Anything in life of value takes time to cultivate.

The real secret to mastering an art is to always be learning. Constant practice without a gap is essential. Lack of consistency prevents you from discovering an art. When there is no consistency, nothing is learned. It is like you want to learn how to surf and take one course every three years. Without consistent discipline, it is impossible to acquire skills. Full attention is required to do any action with quality. If you have a disturbed mind or think you know everything already, you cannot do it properly. To make your total effort in each moment is enough. With an empty mind, you make space for creativity to enter you.

It is essential to understand the difference between *diluted effort* and *discipline*. Diluted effort is when you are heading in the wrong direction. In diluted effort, fear arises, and you worry about not achieving or accomplishing something. If your effort is in the right direction, there is no fear of anything. There is only the constant quality of the right practice. There is only Shoshin.

No matter how knowledgeable you become, with a beginner's mindset, you always have fun. Life is never boring when you are curious. You cannot experience both feelings at the same time. The task you do never seems repetitive because there is always something to learn. Believing you are an expert closes your mind and makes you miss opportunities for learning. If you have a beginner's mindset, you are open and curious.

There is a story about a student who visited a Zen master for the first time. The master asked the student if he could pass him an empty glass and a jar of water. The master began to pour the water into the glass. As it became full, he kept pouring, and the glass started to overflow.

The student asked, "What are you doing? The glass is already full!"

The master answered, "This is how your mind is. Full of preconceptions."

When your mind is full of preconceptions, it is impossible to learn. Whatever you do, always remember to empty your glass.

When you are working on a project or an idea, you should keep a Shoshin mindset. Sometimes you get stuck in your thoughts and are unable to see past them. This is a sign of a closed mentality. By keeping a Shoshin mindset, your projects and ideas are going to grow exponentially. They are not going to be fixed on a specific outcome. They will keep evolving, making them fun and exciting to be a part of.

When I teach yoga and movement, the first thing I tell my students is that they will never be good in my class. As soon as they become good at something, I always change the rules and keep challenging them. This creates many positive outcomes. I am developing my students' character in the same way I developed mine. First, becoming friends with frustration changes a goal-oriented perspective into an exploratory one. Second, a practice full of curiosity makes it exciting. Third, understanding that the learning process itself is a privilege because it is an everlasting one.

When your mind is wandering around, there is no chance for expression. Your freedom is in the very beginning of acquiring skill—not at the end. Do not see discipline as something you need to do in order to get something in return. Being ready to learn is discipline. Learning is an act of liberation. Shoshin makes you free from suppression. Discipline is a vehicle for expression. Discipline gives you freedom! Something I see all the time is when my students develop more skills, they enjoy their bodies even more. For example, when I teach them how to do a handstand, it opens a world of possibilities they did not even know existed. As Epictetus said, "It is impossible for a man to learn what he thinks he already knows." To express your uniqueness, you need the right mix of discipline plus a beginner's mindset.

Another benefit of Shoshin is that constantly learning new skills affects the brain, which is similar to how exercise affects the body. In recent studies, scientists have found that learning new skills is associated with developing gray matter in the brain. Developing gray matter improves control over your five senses. It also helps in decision-making, improves memory, and enhances self-control.

Every time you learn something, your neurons make new connections. Think of learning as getting an upgrade. Shoshin constantly upgrades your brain. It is important to understand what is driving your behavior. For example, we all have a friend who is constantly on a diet. They are always putting diluted effort by counting calories, trying new exercises, or even taking supplements. Because they do not understand the root of their actions, they keep running in circles. They spend so much time and energy fighting against their own programming. By changing your subconscious programming, you no longer need to apply any effort. Everything becomes second nature. This is why I do not believe in the phrase "working hard." You can work harder than anyone, but if you do not understand why you are acting like you do and do not update your programming, your effort will only backfire. You will live a restricting, frustrating, and exhausting life. In a later chapter, you will learn how to fulfill your desires with the least effort necessary (an old yogic secret).

When I was living in Los Angeles, going to the office took a lot of effort. I would find any excuse not to go. Yet, for some reason, being in shape and eating right was always easy. My partners were precisely the opposite. They loved being in the office, but they could not eat healthy even if you paid them. So, I began questioning why, things are easy for some people and not for others. This is when I found that your programming creates your limitations. I only needed to update my software from a limited belief.

Now, I do not use phrases like "I have to do something" or "I have to struggle to achieve anything." By having a Shoshin mindset, I am always learning, growing, and having fun. As Shunryu Suzuki remarks, "In the beginner's mind, there are many possibilities, but in the expert's, there are few."

Do not make the mistake of closing your mind and thinking there is nothing new to learn. In each moment, life presents limitless possibilities for enjoyment and evolution. Approach life with a Shoshin mindset! Be curious and follow whatever you are interested in. And once you acquire a basic skill, be more curious because that is where the fun begins. Please understand the only effort you need to put in is to change your subconscious programming. Action should be enjoyable. I guarantee that you will enjoy aspects of life that you did not even know existed. If you are not enjoying your activity, update your software—and let your subconscious work for you! Because discipline brings you freedom.

ENVIRONMENT, ENVIRONMENT, ENVIRONMENT

PEOPLE USUALLY TEND TO BLAME GENETICS FOR ANY PROBLEM that arises in their bodies. They say things like, "It is difficult for me to lose weight because my mom has always struggled with hers" or "I have a temper because it runs in my family." You are inclined to blame your genes, which makes you believe you are a victim of heredity. The DNA you have is like the blueprint of a building. It establishes some ground rules like eye color, height, and sex. You cannot change the color of your eyes or how tall you are. It is like when you play chess. You can move the pieces however you want, but always according to the rules of the game. Similarly, this is the body you were given. It has genetic information that makes the ground rules. However, how you move your pieces, which is the environment your cells live in, determines how you are going to experience life. When you blame your genetics for health problems, you are putting your attention on the blueprint instead of how you want to construct the building. Building something on a solid foundation is critical for the structure to be as tall as you want it to be. Put yourself in the right environment so your genes can thrive.

Believing that your genes control your life takes away the opportunity of being the alchemist of your body. Scientists have found that single-gene disorders such as Huntington's or cystic fibrosis only affect 2 percent of the population. For the other 98 percent of the world, disease happens because of a deprived environment. As Bruce Lipton, a world-class biologist, explains in his study about cells' behavior: "When I provided a healthy environment for my cells, they thrived; when the environment was less than optimal, the cells faltered. When I adjusted the environment, the sick cells revitalized."

Epigenetics is the science which studies these phenomena. Epigenetics means control above genetics. *Ayurveda* is an ancient yogic science similar to the principles scientists study in epigenetics. In ayurvedic science, the first step of any disease happens due to accumulation. If you live in a constant state of stress and anxiety and do not have a mechanism for relief, it has no choice but to manifest into some kind of disease. Similarly, epigenetics reveals that DNA blueprints passed to genes are not established when you are born. Environmental influences—like nutrition, emotions, stress, overworking, and lack of sleep—modify the gene expression according to the original DNA blueprint. As Joe Dispenza said, "When you change your emotions, you change the expression of your genes because you are sending a new chemical signal to your DNA." Genes do not control your biology—the environment does.

It is impossible to describe an organism without describing its environment. Also, it is impossible to describe an environment without naming the organism that lives in it. The environment and the organism have a transactional relationship. There cannot be bees without flowers or flowers without bees. The flower is the environment for the bee, and the bee is the organism for the flower.

So, who creates the environment in your body? You do! Your thoughts and emotions transmit signals to your cells, producing hormones, chemicals, and all kinds of stuff that alter your body's biology. If you live in constant fear, you are naturally on alert for any potential danger and in continual tension. Fear makes you live believing you need to defend yourself from some external threat. Your system naturally activates stress hormones like cortisol, adrenaline, and noradrenaline because it is in the blueprint of your DNA. If your primal ancestors were being chased by a predator, their bodies would quickly send all the available energy to their arms and legs so they would be able to escape. Your body does not know the difference between psychological and physical fear. By living in a state of fear, you create a destructive environment that manifests into some type of disease.

When you are in an environment of vigilance, sending energy into your digestive system, killing some infection or regenerating new healthy cells will be secondary. Because what would be the point of digesting your food if a lion ate you? It was not your genes that activated the disease; it was the conditions in which you put them. You are living as if you are a sprinter in the Olympics. When the referee screams, "Ready," you put yourself in position. When the referee screams, "Set," you tense all of your muscles, preparing to take off. However, the "go" never comes. How long do you think an Olympic athlete can stay in this position? Two minutes? Five? Eight? This is how you are living now. There is no "go." There is no release of tension. You keep accumulating stress, so your body has no other option than to manifest it into some type of disease.

Let's suppose you are afraid of not getting the promotion you want at the end of the year. Because you have not analyzed the root cause of your fear, you may think, *What will I tell my wife? Do I have a future in this company? My coworker who started working at the same time as me has already been promoted.* Questions like these are coming to your conscious mind because you believe, deep down, that if you do not get this promotion, you will not be loved.

The root cause of your fear is a sense of inadequacy. If you have not acknowledged your root cause, there is a shortcut you can use. Only ask yourself: Do you know for a *fact* that you are not getting promoted—or is it just your imagination?

When something is disturbing you, you should always ask, How would I feel in the *absence* of my concern? How would my body feel? What about my emotional and mental state? With the absence of your concern, you automatically are going to find some freedom. Put yourself in a state where your concerns are nonexistent. Once you feel that freedom, I invite you to spend the rest of the day in this emotional state. Each time you have any type of worry, always acknowledge that you experience harmony in the absence of concern. You have to recognize the external threat and observe what this situation is revealing inside. What is really creating your stress? Every time you do this, you create the right environment for optimal growth.

When you put yourself in a healthy environment, you experience ease. A healthy environment means that you are not in a constant state of stress. Throughout the day, take the time to breathe and give yourself a pause to decompress consciously. Also, sleep is fundamental for your health. Epigenetics shows elevated emotions like gratitude, love, and compassion signal your body's genes to produce healthy cells. In the right environment, your body activates a system that is responsible for healthy digestion, repairing cells, and producing a relaxed state of mind. This automatically strengthens your immune system and reduces blood pressure. To put it simply, a healthy mind produces health.

Knowing that you can control your genes makes you no longer a victim of heredity. Scientists found that an uplifting belief can heal the body. This is called the *placebo effect*. Your body believes the story your mind creates, and it responds accordingly. Just be careful because just as you can heal yourself with an empowering belief, you can also make yourself sick with a disempowering one. This is called the *nocebo effect*. You are totally responsible for the biology of your body. When you hear someone saying, "I'm angry because my dad was always angry," you can safely respond, "It's not the genes; it's the environment, dude." You are the alchemist of your life.

Noticing that the relationship between an organism and its environment is transactional, let's look at your social life. As a destructive environment affects your physiology, a destructive social environment affects you psychologically. If you are around people who incessantly complain, spread negativity, and believe they are victims of the world, your psyche absorbs their lower vibrations. Negativity is inner pollution. In the wrong environment, you have less energy and complain without even realizing you are doing it. You believe being a victim of circumstances is normal. This is the *social nocebo effect*. The social nocebo effect is when your environment disempowers your life.

Consequently, if you hang around creative, energetic, and grateful people, your psyche absorbs these positive vibrations. This is the *social placebo effect*. The social placebo effect is when your environment empowers your life.

Some people make you feel small, depressed, and anxious, and others make you feel optimistic, creative, and happy. They say that you are a combination of the five people you hang out with the most. This is true! Depending on the environment you are in, you live in heaven or hell. Start noticing who you hang out with. If the environment makes a difference in your body, it is a fact that it makes a difference in your life. Understand you are the master of your destiny, so choose your environment wisely. Choose what you like to do and how you like to spend your time and energy. Let yourself do whatever makes you feel alive. That's the optimal environment. That's your duty. That's your responsibility. That's your dharma.

LIFE IS AN INFINITE GAME

PEOPLE APPROACH LIFE AS IF IT IS A SPORTS GAME. THEY CONSTANTLY compete, wanting to be on top. People always want to win. But who makes the rules of the game? How can you win in love? How can you win in friendship? How can you win in business? How can you win in life? There are two types of games: *finite* and *infinite*. Finite games have established rules and time frames. They have a beginning, middle, and end. Like any sports game, such as basketball or baseball, the rules are set before the match starts. There are players, the ones who agree to play, and referees, the ones who ensure players follow the rules. There are also observers, the people who are watching how the game is played. There is a score, and everyone agrees who is the winner and loser. The purpose is to score more points, goals, or touchdowns than the opposite team. The object is to win, and the game comes to an end when someone has won.

In infinite games, there are known and unknown players. The rules of the game are changing all the time. There are no judges or referees. And the objective is not to win. It is to stay in the game as long as possible. There are no winners or losers. Players can enter or leave at any time, but the game always continues—the rules of an infinite game constantly change to prevent anyone from winning.

Let's take a closer look at an infinite game the majority of us play. Business. You do not know everyone who's playing the game. Companies are regularly opening and closing. Also, employees get hired and fired all the time. Yet, the game of business never stops. The rules are always evolving. For example, California laws are constantly being rewritten to facilitate more businesses to open. They change laws to encourage new companies to enter the game and create laws to prevent someone from winning. That is why, in many countries, it is illegal to have a monopoly. As James Carse writes in his book *Finite and Infinite Games*, "Rules of infinite games are like the grammar of a living language, where those of a finite game are like the rules of a debate." People play business, which is infinite, with a finite mentality.

How can you win in business? Who wins anyway? Does the company that makes more revenue win? Is it the one that makes more profit? Or perhaps the one that has the most employees? Or maybe the one that sells more? But what about the costs? Also, how do you measure this data? In a finite game, everybody agrees that the Lakers won because they scored more baskets in the designated time frame. But who makes up the metrics in business? Which company wins if there are no time frames? What time frame are you using to measure your sales, profits, or revenue in a span of a year? Five years? Ten? The metric you choose to measure your success or failure is arbitrary because you are making up your own rules.

There is no such thing as winning in infinite games. If you approach life with a finite mentality, you try to manipulate it to accomplish some metrics you have created yourself. For example, you want to make $100,000 this year. Why in one year and not in fifteen months? Why $100,000 and not a million? These guidelines are only in your head. Living your life trying to accomplish made-up rules can get you in trouble. First, why are you limiting yourself to these metrics? You set up metrics with a limited perception of how you see the world today. Also, if you reach your goal three months later, does that mean you failed? Why are you approaching life with a finite mindset? How much energy are you wasting on this nonsense? You are acting as a slave to time, trying to achieve some goal, and if you do not get it in the time frame you desire, you believe you have failed. You are making yourself miserable by trying to fulfill your own limited expectations.

Finite games can be played within an infinite one. It is vital to see finite goals as something temporary. When Apple invented the iPhone, they did not stop creating new products because they succeeded with one. Apple has an infinite player mentality. That is why they keep developing new products. Blockbuster had a finite mentality until Netflix knocked them out. Blockbuster wanted to win, but Apple wants to remain in the game.

It is not whether you are on top; it is about growing and evolving. Infinite players enter finite games with the appropriate energy necessary but without the seriousness. They engage the game with a playful attitude. To be playful does not mean that the game is not important. It means you allow for possibilities to emerge. To be serious implies you are looking for a specific conclusion. Why focus on beating or outperforming someone else? Do not make the mistake of seeing your life as a finite game. Play as many finite games as you want within the miraculous game of life. By having an infinite mindset, the pressure of winning is going to evaporate because you realize you have already won.

I HOPE YOU NEVER REALIZE
YOUR POTENTIAL

THE MOST IMPORTANT GAMES IN LIFE ARE INFINITE, LIKE LOVE, friendship, marriage, and parenthood, to name a few. Life itself is infinite. Knowing the type of game you are playing gives you many advantages because you stop wasting energy by taking the wrong approach. It is like if you are training to play basketball by practicing chess. I am not saying chess will not give you any skills, but it will not translate onto the basketball court.

To realize what type of game you are playing, it is essential to look at how you measure the outcome. Infinite games have no real metrics to establish a direct answer. Let's analyze an infinite game that we all play: love. Please tell me the day that you fell in love with your wife. Tell me the exact moment when your best friend became your best friend. When was it? Or tell me, how much you love your mother? It is an impossible question. No metric can measure that.

It is funny how falling in love or trusting someone happens. If you think about it, it is like someone pressed a button and suddenly you love or trust your best friend. There is not a particular incident that made this trust happen. It was the accumulation of experiences that allowed that connection.

There is no measurement to quantify love or trust. Relationships are infinite. So why are you approaching them like they are finite? Approach every relationship without finite expectations. Eliminate the notion that you need something from someone in return. Cultivating relationships with an infinite approach makes lasting, loving, and trusting relationships.

Let's look at how relationships are formed. How is trust actually created. What happens if you spend ten straight hours with a stranger? Would you fall in love with them? Of course not! You might like them, but you are not going to fall in love with them. However, what happens if you consistently spend time with a person? It would naturally evolve into a beautiful connection. Who would you trust more: someone who you spent ten straight hours or someone who is consistently in your life? Life is about consistency and not intensity. The most beautiful relationships take constant maintenance. When you stop watering a plant, it dies. Now, let's look at your body. What would happen if you spent ten straight hours in the gym? Would you see any results that day? Obviously not! But if you spend thirty minutes every day, you will. When you approach life with an infinite mentality, you constantly water the plants of your interests. Infinite thinking compounds the outcome of your actions.

Here's the good news: If you cannot win in love, if you cannot win in business, and if you cannot win in life, this means you cannot lose either! Making the realization that there is no winning or losing takes the pressure away from whatever you are doing. This does not mean that you do not want to be better than you were yesterday. This only means you no longer want to be the best. Because being the best is something you make up. Like, how can you be the best boyfriend? You cannot! But you can have more awareness today than you did yesterday. Increasing your presence makes you more enjoyable and, consequently, a better boyfriend. But not the best because the best does not exist. The best only exists in finite games. You are an infinite one.

People always say, "I hope you realize your potential." Realizing your potential is finite thinking. Your potential is infinite. So, I hope you never realize your potential! When you remove the pressure of finite thinking, you see no winning is possible in any game that truly matters. Stop being busy measuring life and start living it. Stop competing with other people and realize that the most intriguing way to spend your time is to be the broadest version of yourself. An infinite mindset gives a tremendous amount of creativity. Not only does it take the pressure off of pursuing made-up metrics, but it also creates a space for expression.

With an infinite mentality, you do the task at hand to the best of your ability—without the pressure of achieving a goal. It does not take your responsibility away. It makes you responsible for everything because life is about consistency and not intensity. When you redefine how you play the game of life, you redefine what you call work. Finite players work, and infinite players play.

One of my closest friends is a writer and was asked to write an article about a subject she did not find interesting. I was talking on the phone with her, and she said, "I do not want to start this project."

We reframed the task in her mind from work to play. As soon as she realized this was just finite thinking, work disappeared from her mind—and she enjoyed the job. The moment you reframe "I have to do something" to "I choose to do something" is the moment you move from finite to infinite thinking. As the brilliant philosopher Alan Watts said, "This is the real secret of life—to be completely engaged with what you are doing in the here and now. And instead of calling it work, realize it is play."

Infinite players are fully committed and totally unattached. In my opinion, this is one of the most powerful ways to approach life. Whatever game you decide to play, let it be about creating joy and happiness for yourself and others. Approach your body with an infinite mentality. Approach love. Approach friendship. Approach life. Approach everything! Even if you play a finite game, know that you are playing a game within a game. Would you consider yourself as winning in life? Winning is not how well you are doing financially, being in a relationship, or whatever definition you are pursuing. Winning is how good you feel about living.

LIFE IS SETTING ME
UP FOR SUCCESS

YOU LIVE YOUR LIFE ACCORDING TO YOUR BELIEFS, AND THE SUM of your beliefs creates your conditioning. Your programming runs your day-to-day life. It shapes your thoughts, words, and actions. These programs contain all of the assumptions about who you are, how you act in the world, and what you expect from yourself, other people, and from life.

Each person has different models installed and perceives the world uniquely. Whatever you have installed, you perceive it as real. Do you even know what models are running your life? These models are not linear. For example, you can have empowering models for running your business but disempowering ones about how to have a loving relationship. Here is the good news: Your beliefs are not you! You can change them whenever they are not serving you. The first step to improving your experience of life is to increase awareness. When you become aware of disempowering models, you can exchange them for empowering ones. Remember, you only need the discipline to exchange them. Once you do, everything becomes effortless. Whatever you are perceiving as a struggle is only revealing an area of your life that is running on a limited model. Replacing old programs is essential.

Fear-based models limit your experiences of life by making you feel anxious, worried, and unhappy. In contrast, love-based models allow you to experience joy, creativity, and freedom. There is always an option to change your behavioral models. When you buy an iPhone, even if it is not the newest model, you constantly update the software. As Tony Robbins says, "Our beliefs are like unquestioned commands, telling us how things are, what's possible and impossible, and what we can and cannot do. They shape every action, every thought, and every feeling that we experience." Updating your programming is the most effective and fastest way to grow in any area of your life because you are going to the root of what is making you think, speak, and act the way you do.

I want to share my own experience of how my life became a nonstop ride of joy. I was living in Beverly Hills with my three best friends. I had a girlfriend, and we had a wonderful relationship. I drove a Mercedes, and I was able to travel all over the world. However, there were many nights that I could not sleep. I noticed my thoughts made me anxious because I constantly thought about what could go wrong with the deal I just closed. I had a goal-orientated life. I was working long hours without a compass, achieving one goal after another. My previous model made me believe that the only way I could be successful was to work harder than anyone else. I started to observe my surroundings to find out if my anxieties were a matter of positioning. I quickly noticed that the owners who made millions of dollars and their employees who were making a yearly salary had the same fears and anxieties as I did. So, clearly, it is not about what position you are in or how much money you make. It is about how you perceive whatever is happening.

Here was my predicament: I was aware that making more money and working long hours did not necessarily make me happy. But this was the programming installed in my subconscious, and it was still running my life. Once I started increasing awareness and exchanging limited belief systems, my life took me in a direction I could not even dream of. Three major realizations helped me uncover my true self. The first was to understand that I am not the voice in my mind. I am not my thoughts; I am the witness of them. The second was that my subconscious programming ran my behavior. So, I can exchange them as I wish. And the third is that life is setting me up for success.

Here are the insights I realized and live by: My life's circumstances are aligning for my own benefit. Everything is working in my favor. Literally, every situation that I encounter is teaching me something. From breaking up with my girlfriend, changing professions, or moving to another country, every experience I have had is part of my learning and happening for my evolution. Whenever something "bad" happens, I look at it and say, "Wow, I wonder what life is teaching me now." The situations I do not understand, instead of classifying them as "good" or "bad," I experience them fully, knowing they are tailor-made for me.

In my world, nothing happens randomly. There is no such thing as coincidences. Everything happens to support my victory. There are no errors; there are only lessons. There are no mistakes; there are only opportunities. Living with the model of deep trust in the universe's perfection allows me to be fully present because I know that I am where I have to be. I know that things just do not happen; they happen *just*. Life always gives me what I need. If you pay attention, everything that happens is a form of teaching. The problem comes when you live on autopilot. When you recycle experiences, the universe presents you with the same teaching until you learn it and for your own sake. It does not matter if it is true or not because it is the way I see the world; I live my life with love and trust. I live in an abundant, loving, harmonious world. And I love it all. The highs and the lows. Existing is a miracle. I am that miracle. Clearly, life is setting me up for success.

Installing deep trust in the universe creates many possibilities. When you stop wasting energy trying to control things, you quit resisting the past. You realize everything that has ever happened to you was for your benefit. This allows you to surrender to the present moment. We all know someone who is trying to control every situation in life, whether it is their business, relationships, and so on. Control steals your attention and energy. Are you really controlling life—or is it just an illusion? Delegating your illusion of control to the universe is the only way you can truly enjoy life. You do it all the time anyway. You delegate the labor of digestion to your system. You eat, and you are not concerned about digesting your food. You know that your body is going to do its job. When you try to control the natural flow of life, you only disturb it. Control makes you feel separate. The way to become one with the universe is to trust it. Realize that controlling is just an old program.

Controlling is the refusal to trust and is limited by your perception. By realizing you are part of life, not apart from life, you automatically delegate authority to the universe. Surrender is what makes you powerful! Do not confuse surrender with giving up. Giving up is saying that you do not care. Surrender is your inner power. It is not to be attached to a specific outcome. Surrendering is using the universe's intelligence for your benefit. It is being receptive to all possibilities. Surrendering is knowing that you can experience joy in every moment. Surrendering does not mean that everything will be all right; it means that everything already is! Surrender is realizing life is setting you up for success.

If you can choose any model, why not choose one that makes you happy? Why not choose one that makes all your dreams come true? As Rumi said, "Live life as if everything is rigged in your favor." Next time someone calls you and says, "I have good news and bad news; which one do you want to hear first?" You can confidently answer, "It does not matter which one you tell me first because both of them are good to me."

The situation you are in—at this moment, whatever it is—is absolutely perfect. There is no error. You did not screw up. Never think that anything is happening *against* you. Everything that happens has the purpose of awakening you. This moment is exactly where you need to be. And understand that to grow inside, you will be challenged in all directions. Instead of looking at these challenges as something negative, these situations should be fun. These challenges are your privilege. Any adversity you face is truly a blessing. Adversity is life setting you up for success.

Once awareness expands, you understand that the best possible experience that *can* happen *will* happen. As Neale Donald Walsch teaches, the universe is sending you nothing but angels! Everything and everyone who has entered your life is for your evolution. Once you truly know this, the way you respond to any situation changes. This happened:

I was helping a friend film his music video. On the second day, there was a scene inside a boat. We drove for two hours to get to the lake. Once we arrived, due to COVID restrictions, they only allowed three people on the boat. So, I said, "You guys go ahead. There is no need for me to go." The moment my friends left, I thought, *Wait a minute. This is not a mistake. This is happening for me.*

I started walking toward town, and I met a guy who told me about an ancient Buddhist temple called the Great Stupa. He said, "Rent a four-wheeler, and I'll take you there."

I rented it and started following the guy up a beautiful mountain. It reminded me of when I lived in Bali and would ride my scooter through the rice fields. When I arrived, it was one of the most gorgeous temples I have ever seen. I meditated for so long that my friends had to wait on me. What an amazing miracle that I was not allowed on the boat!

When I came back to meet my friends, they thought I was on ecstasy. I was so joyful and high on life. Life surprises you when you are open to it. Whenever you are in a situation that is not going as planned, ask yourself, "Why did I bring myself here?" Remember, life is always setting you up for success.

Another insight that happens from a deep trust in the universe is that everything comes at the perfect time. When I truly understood this, it eliminated all the worry in my life. I know things will come when they have to, and they will go away when it's time. Also, it helped me stay present in whatever I am doing because I know I am exactly where I'm supposed to be. I know that the right action will be there when I need it to—not before and not after. If I do not have it yet, I do not need it yet. I stopped trying to control life and started experiencing it. As Mooji says, "Your urge to control life controls you."

Killing my idea of control allows me to be here now. Worry does not exist because I know the whole universe is supporting me. I cannot think of something more fun than genuinely exploring myself. If you really think about it, the smartest thing to do is enjoy the people and circumstances that appear in your life. Life is a process of exploration, not accumulation.

In South Africa, there is an insight known as *Ubuntu*. Ubuntu means "I am because you are." In other words, a person is only a person through other people. I realize that I cannot be all I can be unless you are all you can be. The better you are, the better I am. By adopting this philosophy, I understand that I am where I am supposed to be because everybody else is where they are supposed to be.

A law of the universe is that everything wants to be the broadest version of itself. A grasshopper wants to be the fullest grasshopper it can be. I want to be the best me I can be. To become the best I can be, I need you to be the best you can be. Understanding Ubuntu means that the lack of your best hurts the entire world. It is time you realize life is setting you up for success.

EVERYTHING YOU
DO MATTERS

THERE ARE TWO FUNDAMENTAL MODELS YOU CAN LIVE YOUR LIFE by. The first is that whatever you do is unimportant. You are just a little person on a planet that is part of a vast solar system, part of a galaxy, part of an immense universe. You are only one person in a world that has more than seven billion people. In this model, you try to take as much as you can, as fast as you can, without the concern of harming others because there is no meaning in existing. You can stay at home and watch television or browse social media all day. In model one, there is no responsibility because who cares? The second model is the opposite—everything you do matters. Everything you do is important. Every thought you think, every word you say, and every decision you make creates an infinite effect that alters everything else.

Let's analyze both models. The first one that says everything you do is meaningless seems like it has an advantage because it eliminates your responsibility. Living by this model prevents any chance of enjoyment. You act selfishly, trying to get as much as you can from whomever you can. You act defensively, guarding the limits of your conditioning. You envy people in different positions, always hyper-focused on what you are lacking. You perceive a hostile world where everyone is separate and competitive. Because of this, you are not compassionate to yourself or others. Why would you be? This model makes you think you are here by mistake; therefore, you lose the ability to enjoy the miracle of life.

The second model says *everything* you do matters. This makes you responsible for everything. You are in the center of a network. Every person meets at least a thousand people. So, when two people meet, it impacts a million people. And when three people meet, it impacts a billion people. That is how we are all connected. The things you do affect everyone in the network. Every decision you make creates a ripple effect, and it travels outward, affecting things you cannot fully comprehend. The things you do or do not do are far more important than you can imagine. Think about it, if your great-grandparent had been angry the day he met your great-grandmother, you would not be here. Actions affect the lives of people around you and have a direct or indirect effect on people now and generations to come.

Every decision you make affects the whole world. When I began to operate from this framework and started to experience a world of joy and possibility, people around me automatically began reaching out to ask my secret. This was when I decided to teach my discoveries.

One of my closest friends, a musician, was having problems communicating with his producer while recording his new album. As we started working with his consciousness, he realized that he was living by a limited model. He was acting defensively because he was taking everything his producer said personally. Once we got to the root of his concerns, we removed the limited perception that made him believe he had a problem. Whatever was happening was one thing, and how he perceived it was another.

At first, he thought his producer was unfair. But later, he realized the producer was doing the best he could with his level of awareness and behaving based on his programming. This is how it usually works. Once you stop taking things personally, you can start becoming compassionate toward yourself and others. As soon as his awareness expanded, he naturally increased his vibrational rate because he focused on what he wanted—recording the best album—instead of what he was lacking, complaining about the "unfairness" of his producer.

When this happened, the producer started acting differently. He opened up to him and said he was having marital trouble. Once they talked about it, they focused on finishing the album, and it is the best one they have created yet. The cool thing was when my friend increased his awareness, not only had an improved relationship with his producer, but his producer also improved his relationship with his wife.

Everything you do affects everything else in ways you cannot even imagine. By increasing my awareness, I improved my life, and I was able to help my friend, and he was then able to help his producer, who was able to improve his relationship with his wife. I have never met the producer, but that is the ripple effect. I do not know how many people benefit from the producer and his wife having a better relationship, but for sure, it is more than one person. And that person will affect other people. One of the most significant insights you can learn is to realize and constantly remember that everything you do matters.

Living in model one may look easier because you have no

responsibility toward yourself or others. You are a victim of life with no power, meaning, or accountability. Lack of purpose makes you feel meaningless. It is like being a prisoner who does not even know he is in jail. People who live under model one may think that not having any responsibilities makes them free. In reality, not being responsible for your thoughts, words, and actions makes you a slave. The day you become 100 percent responsible for yourself is when freedom and purpose appear in your life. Freedom equals responsibility. To measure how meaningful and liberated your life is, measure how responsible you are for your own being. And by the way, if you think the world is meaningless, by definition, your statement is also meaningless.

When you understand everything you do matters, it makes you fully conscious about the impact you have in your life, on the people surrounding you, and on the people surrounded by the people surrounding them. It makes you responsible for your life, which consequently gives you meaning.

Each of your thoughts, words, and actions affects the whole network. *Everything* you do matters—from how you say good morning to your neighbor, when you decide not to gossip about your friends, or whenever you want to judge someone, pay them a compliment instead—and see what happens. If you have an opportunity for growth, take it! Not only for yourself—but for the whole world—recognize the power of your life. Take responsibility because it is your privilege.

THE ECONOMICS OF ENERGY
(LAW OF LEAST EFFORT)

OUR CULTURE TEACHES THAT WORKING HARD IS THE KEY TO success. They say you should study hard, work hard, and love hard. Everything you do, do it hard! No one teaches that you should work joyfully. Nobody says love should be effortless or learning should be fun. Why are you working so hard? You make yourself miserable in the process of working because you believe that working hard is the only way to accomplish anything. If you do not work hard all the time, you think you are lazy and will not succeed. This is simply not true. You live by the misconception that to be successful, you need to postpone your happiness. You work hard today for imaginary rewards in the future. This is really dangerous because working hard does not mean that things will happen the way you want them to.

There are people who seems to always have luck on their side. When I was young, my father and uncle both had jewelry stores one block apart. My father always told me that my uncle had the best luck. Frequently, the big client would end up buying from my uncle even though they each had similar locations and merchandise. They both worked equally hard, but working hard does not guarantee better results. If you look at how nature's intelligence works, you can see it does so without effort. The earth does not put any effort into rotating around the sun. A tree grows, a shark swims, and a bee flies effortlessly. Similarly, your cells know how to regenerate without any conscious effort. Your hair and nails know how to grow, your heart pumps blood throughout your body, and you digest your food naturally. Nature is giving you all the clues to creation. Natural law operates efficiently, using the least amount of effort necessary. Nature loves efficiency; from the cosmos to your cells, everything tends to organize with infinite intelligence and not through hard work.

The law of least effort is based on the fact that nature's intelligence manifests itself without any effort. If you learn how to flow with nature's intelligence, it can work for you, or better, through you. You have an unlimited amount of energy inside yourself, but you often block it because you are in resistance to how things are right now. I am not saying that the situation you are going through is ideal, but it is what it is. Not accepting the way things are creates a blockage between you and nature's intelligence. The more you learn how to stay present, the more energy you can access. When you are worrying or complaining, you are working against the entire universe. So, accepting this moment is fundamental.

Whenever something happened in my uncle's life, he always said, "Don't worry—something better is always going to come." He was using the law of least effort without even knowing it! And guess what? So are you. To access your full intelligence, realize that you have been using it all along. You created all the experiences you have lived until now. When you acknowledge the richness of this moment, you stop worrying and start experiencing the miracle of life. You are a conduit through which all energy flows. Acceptance is the only way to flow with the universe.

The first thing you need to understand is that there is no wrong way to do anything. It is only about being effective or not, depending on what you want to experience. Right and wrong are merely mental constructs. Sometimes you believe you made the wrong choice because the experience you got was not the one you wanted. The universe will match and produce situations for you to experience the concept you have of yourself. The universe works like a mirror. It reflects what you put in front of it. The events in your life are only reflections of who you believe you are in this moment. If you want to build a huge building but only have a small piece of land, it would be physically impossible to build it in that space even if you work nonstop. Similarly, if the concept you have of yourself does not match what you want to experience, it will be impossible for life to give it to you. To use nature's intelligence, you need to expand the concept you have of yourself. You need to expand your land of consciousness so you can build whatever you want.

Expansion of consciousness, as with anything, comes with a price. It eliminates your limitations. Realize that hard work is not going to get you there. You need an expansion of perception and intelligence. The way to access your full intelligence is to look for ways to constantly expand your perception. Acknowledge that the world has no control over you. The world only reflects the concept of who you think yourself to be. Remember, beyond your internal dialogue of limitation is the world of possibilities. Beyond the perception of scarcity is the abundant universe.

Society teaches principles of scarcity. That is why they say you should work hard. A lack of understanding of principles of abundance makes you perceive a world of insufficiency. If you learn how to control your energy, you can operate from an abundant mindset. A scarcity mindset comes from poverty of the mind. A scarcity mindset causes fear, worry, and greed because you think there are limited resources. It causes jealousy because you are looking at the people around you instead of looking at yourself. An abundant mindset causes excitement for expression, curiosity, and joy. The universe has unlimited resources, so opportunities and possibilities are infinite. An abundant mindset allows you to do whatever you do as joyfully and lovingly as possible. As a way to celebrate who you are. Action is always a means of joy. Not as a means of attainment. Cooperate with your destiny. Allow it to fulfill itself. Understand that it takes the same amount of effort to live a life of scarcity as to live an abundant one. Being who you are does not require any effort. Relax—another opportunity is always on its way.

The key to using the law of least effort is by knowing the economics of energy. Negativity prevents the help of nature's intelligence. Whatever you do, if you are pessimistic, the universe will not help you. The entire universe collaborates with you to fulfill a desire born out of compassion and love. When you are in a state of joy, the energy you emit is traveling faster through space. When you are in a state of negativity, the energy you emit travels slower. You can be working as hard as you want, but by emitting low vibrations, you are only working so hard to be the best version of your limited self.

Nothing can happen unless the entire universe makes

it happen. Everything has to collaborate for you to be in this moment. Everything happens according to natural law. A series of possibilities unfolds with your thoughts, words, and actions. You must align your thoughts and emotions to perform a powerful action. You are doing one thing while feeling another and thinking something else. This is not very powerful, is it? A strong seed gives life to a tree even in the desert, and a weak seed will not grow even in favorable conditions. When your thoughts, feelings, words, and actions are in sync, you use the economics of energy to connect with nature's intelligence. Everything aligns in the direction of your will. You notice synchronicities. You meet the right people and go through the right circumstances. You experience perfect timing. You will be like my uncle making the big sale without necessarily working harder. Luck is only living under cosmic guidance.

Your body is an energy-management device. But where does this energy come from? Where do your ideas originate? Ideas are floating as forms of energy. They want to be expressed in the world. When you get an idea, know that you are working with it. The idea is using you, and you are using the idea. It is a partnership. As in any partnership, if you do not act on it, it will go away. When you get an idea and work with it, you are using the law of least effort. The universe is recruiting you as the device for expression. Do not worry about how you will manifest it. The universe will present the plan along the way. However, the universe is forced to respect your mental boundaries. It cannot give you something you do not believe you deserve.

David Lynch compares grabbing creative ideas to catching big fish. On the surface, there are only small fish. The big ones live at the bottom. Similarly, on the surface of your mind are the mechanical ideas. The creative ones live in deeper layers. If you want to catch the big fish, you need to quiet your mind and listen. In other words, the more conscious you are, the bigger net you have to catch more creative fish.

Taoism teaches an insight called *Wu Wei*. Wu means no, and Wei means forcing. It is the principle of effortless action. For example, one of my friends is a professional fighter. Physically, I am taller and stronger than him, but when we wrestle, I always get tired faster because I am tensing all of my muscles. He uses his body's intelligence and only applies strength when he has to. He is practicing Wu Wei, while I am not. My body is working harder than his, but he always beats me.

Wu Wei is about knowing when to take the right action. Wu Wei is living life as the art of sailing instead of rowing. If you are working so hard while getting minimal results, know you are rowing. Have you ever noticed that anxious and unsatisfied people are always busy? As Tim Ferris said, "Being busy is a form of laziness. Lazy thinking and indiscriminate action. Being selective, doing less, is part of being productive."

When you are always busy, you are engaging in *compulsive action*. Compulsive action is not working with the flow of the universe because you are constantly reacting. People avoid painful emotions by staying busy. They use compulsive action as an escape. People who are always busy are afraid of looking at themselves. Conscious activity is action, not reaction. Action is always good; reaction is always limited. In conscious activity, you are using the economics of energy to fulfill your desires. You are acting by intelligence rather than effort. This does not mean you are a couch potato. Ceasing to do things does not make you actionless. Because what is the point of being busy on the wrong things? Always act—don't react! Your growth should be natural, not painful. Working hard is an inefficient way to make your desires a reality. When you are overworked, you tend to be stressed and anxious. You automatically are less efficient because you are exhausted, and every step is difficult. Many scientific studies say happiness is the new productivity. So, by being happy now, instead of working to be happy later, you are using the law of least effort.

People like to complicate their lives to be entertained. They tend to make simple things complicated and then call themselves smart. Making a complex thing simple is intelligence—not the other way around. Alan Watts introduced the backward law: the more you pursue something reinforces the fact that you lack it in the first place. The more you desperately want to be rich, the poorer you will feel regardless of how much money you already have. Your attention is on what you do not have, and your pursuit creates resistance.

The energy of wanting to overcome your failures only reinforces the fact that you failed. You already are what you are trying to become. The more you try, the more you miss. I see this phenomenon all the time. When I teach yoga, and one of my students is trying really hard to stretch a particular muscle, the more he tries, the less he stretches. The more efficient way is to relax and let your body do whatever it needs to do.

The secret of yoga, like the secret of creation, is not to force it. This happens to people who cannot sleep. The more they try to sleep, the less they actually sleep. Sleeping happens naturally. When you let go, everything works as it should. You need to get out of your own way. When an idea comes to you, you are working with it to manifest it. Know that the whole cosmos is behind you. It should not take any effort. This does not mean you will not put energy into it. This means that the activity you do is part of your enjoyment. You do not need to know how everything is going to happen. And why would you? Better enjoy the mystery of your creation and see where it takes you. And remember, use your imagination and not your willpower.

To use the law of least effort, you need to use your full intelligence, which is interconnected with nature's intelligence. Let's connect the three facets of your intelligence so you can use this law: the power of your subconscious mind, the power of your attention, and the power of your vibration. The law of least effort is when your subconscious mind works for you, your attention is focused on what you want to create, and the frequency of your vibrations is in alignment with your desires. It is funny how nature responds to all three facets of your intelligence with the same method. The method is *feeling*. Feeling is the method of passing information to your subconscious mind. It is the way of creating the energy of having. Feeling is the system of uplifting your vibrations. Remember if there is something you wish to experience, do not want it—choose it!

When your actions are motivated by love, the universe gives you everything you need. The fabric of the universe is love. So, by definition, any action motivated by love is working with nature's intelligence. You can also see in nature that there are seasons, and flowers always bloom at the right time. Your only job is to plant seeds of love, gratitude, and abundance, and they will bloom at the right time. You are here to live an abundant life. It is your birthright. The more you work with or through the universe, the more abundant your life is. When you use the law of least effort, you use nature's intelligence to experience anything you want.

True wealth is being able to create and experience whatever you have inside your heart. It is nature's job to give you everything you need. It gives bees pollen and water for the trees to grow. Ideas are your pollen, and they come via your intuition. When you are too busy trying to control life, there is no space for creativity. Acceptance and nonresistance are the paths to use nature's intelligence. Even though you would like things to be different in the future, you need to be in harmony with this moment. When you are in harmony with the way things are, you can access a space of creativity and manifest any desire inside your heart. Learn the economics of energy so you can use the law of least effort.

LIVING IN A WORLD OF FULL POSSIBILITIES

THE KYBALION IS THE STUDY OF HERMETIC PHILOSOPHY. HERMES Trismegistus was known as the master of masters in both ancient Egypt and Greece. The origins of his teaching go way back before Moses. Historians have even suggested that Abraham, the father of the Old Testament, learned his mysticisms from Hermes. His first and most fundamental lesson is this: "The all is mind; the universe is mental."

The *Yogacara* is a philosophical system from Mahayana Buddhism, which points to the same teaching: "The world is mind only" (*cittamatram lokam* in Sanskrit). In other words, consciousness is the only reality. What you see as objects, people, and circumstances are the products of your own consciousness. Anything you can imagine, such as wealth, health, or wisdom, manifests as a product of your own mind. The concept you have of yourself is the way you create the world. If the concept of yourself were different, everything in your reality would be different.

Once you truly understand that consciousness is the only reality, you automatically get free from the illusion that something out there, besides your mind, can affect your life. Circumstances happen as a result of consciousness. So, if you want to change your circumstances, you have to expand your consciousness. Remember, there is no separation between you and consciousness. You are it. This means that all you have and will experience is your own creation. What happens is that sometimes the gap between the created and the creation is long enough that you forget that you created this situation in the first place. Once you understand your own power, you can play around with it. The formula is really simple: The time it takes to see your beliefs as facts is the time it takes for your desires to be experienced.

Everything you do is a statement of who you are. Whatever you do, ask—is this aligned with the version of myself I want to experience? The more aligned you are, the better you feel. The universe never says no to your beliefs. It only magnifies them. Your limit comes when you act from a place of fear. It also comes from a lack of attention, which translates to a lack of belief.

Affirmations do not work from a place you want to create results. Every time you say, "I will be," it is an energetic statement that *you are not*! Affirmations only work from a place where the results have already happened. Whatever you say after "I am" is what you are going to end up experiencing. Notice the difference between the energetic statement of "I want to be successful" and "I am successful." In the first, you see yourself as wanting. In the second, you see yourself as successful. As Neville said, "Make your future dream a present fact." You already are what you want to become. It is only your refusal to believe it that prevents you from experiencing it.

The universe works in perfect geometry. The earth rotates around the sun because it found its balance. You work the same way. If you can align the full power of your consciousness, you can be in balance and find perfect geometry within yourself and live in a state of harmony. As you know, your behavior is based on your conditioning, and the way you perceive the world is written in your subconscious programming. When you align the power of your subconscious mind, the power of your attention, and the power of your vibration, you experience abundance. The concept you have of yourself is how you are using your geometry to experience the world.

Sleep is the most accessible door into your subconscious. Your subconscious mind is more susceptible to accept information when you emit alpha brain waves. When you produce melatonin, your brain waves slow down automatically from beta to alpha. Before you go to sleep and as soon as you wake up are the best times to send conscious impressions to your subconscious mind.

Be aware that when you produce stress hormones, your melatonin levels decrease. When you experience stress, you do not have the power to influence your subconscious and access the intelligence of your full consciousness. Do not sleep with worry in your mind. Do not sleep with the feeling of failure. Sleep feeling that things are as you wish them to be. When you go to sleep every night, feel satisfied. Rest in the belief that you are the source of everything you want to experience. Sleep *feeling* that you lack nothing.

What the future holds only depends on the state of consciousness you are in right now. And remember, *feeling* and *persistence* are essential for influencing your subconscious mind and expanding the concept you have of yourself.

Close your eyes and think of the highest thought you have

ever dared to think about yourself. Hold this image as your truth. Start experiencing your life from this space. Notice how you feel physically, emotionally, and spiritually. From this place, you lack nothing.

Spend as long as you can living in your highest truth. When you forget and feel uneasy, remember you can always come back. Hold your highest concept as your truth.

Write this down, place it next to your bed, read it before you go to sleep, and as soon as you wake up:

- I am here to express and experience the highest concept I have of myself.
- I am the source of whatever I want to experience.
- I am the source because I can give to others what I want to experience. If I can give it to others, it means I already have it.
- I lack nothing.

Constant reminders:

- The world is working in my favor.
- Being present makes me powerful.
- Surrender makes me powerful.
- The circumstances of my life are aligning for my benefit.
- I am extraordinary.
- I am responsible.
- I am in harmony with everything as it is right now.
- I am fully committed and totally unattached.
- I play the game of life entirely—without any attachment to the outcome.

- My success is measured by how joyful I am.
- I live life as if everything is rigged in my favor.
- I live in a world where there are no errors.
- Everything I do matters.
- The lack of my best hurts the entire world.
- It is my job to bring happiness into the world.
- Every day is a celebration.
- I have a great destiny.
- Life is setting me up for success.

Close your eyes and feel:

- Every cell in my body is love.
- Every cell in my body is abundant.
- Every cell in my body is in harmony.
- Every cell in my body is open to receive.

And don't forget … this is a dream! Enjoy it!

BE HERE NOW

I LOVE HOW EVERYONE ALWAYS SAYS, "STAY IN THE PRESENT" OR "Be in the moment." This is implying that you have a choice. Have you ever been somewhere else than where you are right now? If you can time travel, this statement would be valid. But you have no choice. You are always here—in the eternal now.

You usually miss the present because you are in resistance to the past or worried about the future. The paradox is when you face the future, you are thinking about the future as well! When have you been in the future? Your life is a series of here-and-now moments, one after another. When the future comes, it comes as the present. By being anxious about it, you are sowing seeds of worry in your mind and creating the habit of worry. This habit will make you anxious your entire life. As Marcus Aurelius, a Roman emperor and Stoic philosopher, wrote in his journal: "Never let the future disturb you. You will meet it, if you have to, with the same weapons of reason which today arm you against the present." Live intensely and totally in the moment because the next moment is born out of this one.

You say you want peace of mind, but what you really want is peace *from* mind. When the mind is under control, you can be present enjoying this moment. When it is not, you start trying to predict the future or holding on to something that already happened. Let's analyze how a typical day works: You wake up. Your body feels healthy. You eat breakfast. You start your car, and no engine lights come on. You arrive at work safely, and you say what's up to your coworker. You have a productive day at work, but on the way home, a car cuts you off in traffic. Instantly, you get angry and scream, "Who taught this guy how to drive?" All the blessings that happened throughout your day are not in your consciousness anymore. When you arrive home, you see your wife, and the first thing you tell her is about the guy who cut you off in traffic. Your attention is 100 percent focused on what went "wrong."

You forget everything has to collaborate with you in order for you to do anything. All your focus is on the one thing you did not like that happened. First, how do you know that the guy who cut you off in traffic did not prevent an accident? Second, you focus on the one thing that went "wrong" and not on everything that went right. You have so many blessings around you, every second that you are alive, yet you focus on whatever you believe is not working. When one tooth hurts, you notice it the whole day, but you cannot even feel them when your teeth are healthy. Do not lose the only thing you have: this moment.

There is an answer to all of your problems. This answer is so powerful that it can release all your anxieties instantaneously. You may worry about how much your company will sell this quarter, if your ex-girlfriend is going to call you, or if your son will be accepted into a particular school. If you are really sincere with yourself, the answer to all of your worries is really simple. The most genuine answer is this: "I don't know."

It is impossible to know what is going to happen next. There are too many variables. When you understand that you don't know what will happen next, you access the power of the present moment. Being okay with not knowing makes you powerful because uncertainty is a law of the universe. *I don't know* exterminates the fictitious future. *I don't know* is not a negative statement. Every discovery has come from this understanding. Only from a space of presence can you access a world of creativity. Change can only happen now—never in the future.

Why are you so obsessed with the future anyway? The idea that you know what you will do in a week or three years is simply stupid. Your brain's function is to attend to the present moment with all its capabilities and not to send you wondering about your desires in the future. The only way you can enjoy life is by acknowledging that you don't know what will happen.

All the ancient texts and all the masters throughout history teach the same insight: Be here now. Do not let your mind take control of your life. Do not let your mind wonder about the past or the future. Stress is caused by being here and yearning to be somewhere else. The *here* seems like it is never good enough, so you keep losing the now. Buddha said, "The past is already gone—the future is not yet here. There's only one moment for you to live."

Lao Tzu wrote, "If you are depressed, you are living in the past. If you are anxious, you are living in the future. If you are at peace, you are living in the present."

Seneca said, "Life is very short and anxious for those who forget the past, neglect the present, and fear the future."

When I was studying yogic philosophy, my teacher, Surinder

149

Singh, said, "The past: emotion, the future: passion, now: compassion." No matter the time in history—no matter the teacher or the school of thought—they all have the same message. You cannot be free in the future. Being present is the master key to your freedom.

People want to know what is going to happen in their lives. Some use astrological horoscopes, and others read palms or tarot cards. Can the stars, your hand, or any card tell you what will happen in the next four minutes? Of course not! Isn't it wonderful that despite all the technology in the world, you do not know what the next moment is going to bring? Not knowing what is going to happen is a blessing.

Let's say your favorite director is coming out with a new suspense movie. All your favorite actors are in it. Would you like me to tell you the ending—or would you rather watch it? Usually, when an unexpected twist happens, you leave the theater saying, "Wow, what a great movie!" But if everything is predictable, you tend to get bored and might even leave the theater early. Similarly, in your life, if things do not go according to plan, isn't this exciting? Why would you want to live your life like the boring, predictable movie that you left the theater early for? The only thing that is happening is that you lost the ability to enjoy the suspense. Not knowing what is going to happen is what makes life worth living. Why do you want to know the score before the game starts? Any game where the results are known is not worth playing. You can see this in chess. When a player knows that it is inevitable for their opponent to win, they forfeit and start another.

You can only experience reality when your mind is not wandering around. The question is: Are you experiencing life from moment to moment—or are your anxieties stealing your moment to moment? As Sadhguru said, "If you know how to deal with what's now, you know how to deal with your entire life!"

Every time you notice your mind wandering around, just remember to *be here now*. You came here to experience life—not to predict it or run away from it. The past comes in the form of guilt, and the future comes in the form of worry. Neither of them exists. Realize that you do not have a choice to be somewhere else—so you might as well enjoy the ride.

NOW, YOGA

Whether you know it or not, you exist as a part of everything else. You think there is you, and then there is the universe. Your individuality makes you experience the world as separate, yet you are connected to the rest of existence. The oxygen you inhale, the trees exhale, and what you exhale, the trees inhale. Who you believe yourself to be is just a mental boundary.

The word yoga means union. Yoga is expanding your consciousness and realizing that you are one with everything and everyone else in the universe. *The Yoga Sutras of Patanjali* is one of the most profound documents in yogic science. This type of yoga is called Raja Yoga, or the eight limbs. The eight limbs are a method that Patanjali developed scientifically to expand your individuality and experience the bliss of oneness. He calls it *Samadhi*, but you can call it *enlightenment* as well.

Patanjali codified yoga with 196 sutras. Sutra, in Sanskrit, means minimal words. The first sutra begins with a really simple line: "Now, Yoga!" Yoga is not just twisting your body while balancing on your head. Asanas, or physical postures, are just one aspect of the eight limbs. As Sadhguru said, "Just teaching the physical aspect of yoga … is not only inefficient; it is a tragedy."

Yoga is now. Yoga is the inner technology to help you create a distinction between you and your thoughts. Every time you are enjoying this moment, you are being a yogi.

There are different paths you can take to experience the oneness of the universe within yourself. Jnana Yoga uses the mind, Karma Yoga uses action, Bhakti Yoga uses the heart, and Raja Yoga uses the eight limbs. If you are attracted to Zen, you use the mind to transcend the mind. This is Jnana Yoga. The Yoga of the intellect. If your heart is devoted to God, you are using Bhakti Yoga. The Yoga of devotion. If you use your work as your spiritual practice, this is Karma Yoga. The Yoga of selfless action. Raja Yoga uses the eight limbs to expand your consciousness scientifically, including physical postures, pranayama (breathing exercises), concentration, and meditation. They are all complementary, so why not use them all? Use Jnana Yoga to sharpen your intellect. Use Karma Yoga to make you efficient. Use Bhakti Yoga to open your heart. Use Raja Yoga to strengthen your mind and body. Yoga is experiencing joy. God is infinite potential.

Any individual who transcended into a deeper state of consciousness came back with the same message. If you read Jesus, Bob Marley, or Neil deGrasse Tyson, they all say the same thing. Jesus said, "There is neither Jew nor Greek … there is neither male nor female for you are all one." Bob Marley sang, "One love, one heart … As it was in the beginning, one love. So, shall it be in the end, one heart." Or, as astrophysicist Neil deGrasse Tyson says, "We are all connected; To each other, biologically. To the earth, chemically. To the rest of the universe atomically."

Truth is one. Teachers express it in many ways. At the deepest truth, all methods are not in contradiction. When you are busy with your problems, you identify with your beliefs. Yoga is the science for expanding your individual consciousness into cosmic consciousness. Yoga is a science, not a faith. It's a tool, not a dogma. As Swami Satchidananda said, "Yoga is not a religion, but it can help you understand your own religion by showing what is fundamental to all great religions." When you experience oneness, you awaken to the illusion that you are a separate being. This has been proven scientifically in quantum physics (more on this later!).

If you go to a concert, the people in the first row have a different viewpoint than the people in the corner and from the people backstage. Yoga is when you stop focusing on where you are sitting and recognize there is a cosmic show right in front of you. When you complain, you miss the show. This is why Patanjali's first sutra is "Now, Yoga." If you are concerned about the past or future, it is impossible to enjoy the show and dance with the universe. The show is always now. The point of existing is to be playful. Existence is like music. You do not work the guitar; you play it. The whole purpose of playing it is to play.

People say life is a journey... no it's not! The point of any trip is to arrive at a destination. If you believe that life is a journey, you think life has a serious purpose in the end. That the point of your existence is to get there, call it success, fame, or wealth. Society trains you to go from preschool to middle school, high school, and college. Then, to get a job and try to achieve some quota of success. You are always trying to get there. Saying life is a journey is looking at life as a pilgrimage. Yet, when you get there, you still feel separate because life is not a journey. It's not a pilgrimage. There is no destination. Yoga is a reminder that life is like music. The purpose of life is to dance and celebrate. This is why yogis refer to the universe as *Lila*. Lila in Sanskrit means divine play. Notice the difference between a game and a play. A game needs a purpose, a result, something to achieve. If you go to a sports game, the purpose is to see your team win. In a play, like in music, there is no goal attached to it. You do not go to a concert or a theater to see who wins. You go to enjoy, sing, dance, and celebrate. The purpose of life is to play without an attachment to the outcome. If you are attached, you are missing the show. Yoga is not against pleasure; on the contrary, once you taste the bliss of being one with the whole universe, small treats become tasteless.

What would happen if everything that you thought was wrong is actually right? You always think your perception is right—and others are wrong. Self-righteousness is shared because you see the world through the lens of your conditioning. You did not choose where you were born. If it happened to be in America in the 1970s, you thought the Northern Vietnamese were the enemy. In the same way, if you were born in North Vietnam, you believed America was the enemy. Because you identify yourself with your conditioning, you cannot listen to what all the teachers from all aspects of human knowledge are saying. Righteousness blocks effective action because it prevents you from understanding. Compassion and righteousness can never come together. If you are trying to be right, you are losing your compassion. Yogis call righteousness the golden chain. It is the last gate to access your inner temple, which means total freedom. A golden chain could be really nice because it is made out of gold, but it is still a chain! The game is to be free—not to be right.

Let's say four blindfolded men are touching an elephant. One is touching the legs, another the ears, another the trunk, and another the belly. They think that the part of the elephant they are touching is the whole elephant. Throughout history, people have been fighting to defend their conditioning, trying to prove that their part of the elephant is the whole truth. Yoga is taking the blindfold off and seeing the entire elephant.

When I was studying yogic philosophy, one of my teachers was an Indian monk, Swami Atma. He said, "I believe in all the masters because they are all trying to teach compassion." I was moved beyond words because this was the first person I had ever met who did not try to make anyone wrong. Instead, he said everyone was right. This lesson was vital for me to break free entirely from my conditioning. Yoga is like the sun; it gives sunshine to everyone.

Life is energy manifested in different forms. Life separates itself to play. It is like if you go to the park and want to play basketball, you split into two teams. Similarly, your individuality is Lila, divine play. When you forget this, you play the game of life seriously. Competition is enjoyable when you are using it to express and sharpen your skills. When it becomes the goal, it stops being fun, and you can injure yourself and others. When you play in unity, it is always enjoyable.

The yogic game involves two parts. First is finding out how to experience, within your individuality, the unity of all. Secondly, from this place of oneness, it is finding out how to express your individuality by honoring everything you were given, like your body, family, or religion. The secret of creation also works in two parts. First, you have to be in harmony with the way things are. Second, from this liberated space, you can access a world of creativity. Remember, it is nothing but the same energy expressing itself differently. Express who you are for the benefit of all. The most incredible miracle of existence is that we are able to have an individual experience. Honor your individuality by taking care of your body, mind, and actions. So, now, Yoga!

Do you know why yogis say *namaste?* Namaste means the light in me recognizes the light in you. Namaste addresses the source, not the personality or body. The science of yoga is being in perfect alignment with your inner and outer world. Maharishi Mahesh Yogi teaches to live life 200 percent: 100 percent inner and 100 percent outer. Look at a tree. First, the roots have to grow down for it to grow up. The proportion of how deep the roots grow is in proportion to how tall the tree is. Do not miss the chance of enjoying life at 200 percent!

Yoga is the inner technology that helps you download the inner well-being app to sync with the whole universe. As Sadhguru says, "Yoga is not about being superhuman, it is about realizing that being human is super." The effort to know yourself is yoga. It is the process of removing all that you are not. The game is to be awakened from the illusion of separateness. You can only experience oneness when the mind is completely silent, and you raise your individual consciousness into a state of Samadhi.

Now, let's go a little further. What is morality? Everything in the world happens in context. Saying something is absolutely right or absolutely wrong only depends on what side of the coin you are looking at. For example, lying is morally wrong, but if you have to lie to save someone's life, is it? Or stealing is ethically wrong, but if you steal a piece of bread to give to a starving child, is it?

Morality is needed when you feel separate from the rest of existence. Did anybody teach you not to cut yourself? Obviously not! Morality tries to teach you not to harm others, but if you experience others as part of yourself, morality is no longer needed. Morality is ineffective because everything always happens in context. Oneness is the dimension above morality. Once you know that everything is a part of you, you act without imposing moral judgments. When you know that the starving person is a part of you, you give him something to eat naturally. There is no moral responsibility to share. You give because you are giving to yourself. Realize everything is a part of yourself, grow above morality, and share your gift with the rest of existence.

How can you understand something that you have never experienced? If you have never tasted honey, it would be impossible for you to know. I can describe it as sweet or sticky, but even then, you would not know the taste. You need to taste it to find out. In the same way, you cannot understand oneness if you have never experienced it. So, what is a religion, after all? Some masters use words in some way, and others use them in another. Truth is behind and beyond words. To taste truth, you need to experience it.

There are many paths—and all roads lead to Rome. Find out for yourself! Be one with the universe. Just be careful because being addicted to any method is dangerous. Know that you are only trying to know yourself. When you are in equanimity, you reach higher levels of awareness and experience what Swami Atma was teaching me: "Every person who teaches compassion is right."

SOCIETY IS A REFLECTION
OF MYSELF

CAN YOU IMAGINE A WORLD WHERE TRILLIONS OF INDIVIDUALS are living in peace and harmony? This place is called the human body. Your body contains around thirty trillion cells, and they all collaborate to keep you alive. Let's analyze their behavior to see if we can learn something from them.

Cells are flexible and adapt depending on what the body needs. Cells know that every other cell is equally important. Cells function efficiently, using the least amount of energy possible, and they completely trust that the whole provides for them. People do the opposite. They separate according to the society they are born into. Whether it is capitalist or communist, they behave according to their environments, acting in obedience to their background rules. If you identify yourself as Christian, Muslim, or Jewish, you believe this is who you are. It's funny how people say they are their religion, political party, or even their country, such as "I am Jewish," "I am a Republican," or "I am American." They do not say "I believe in Judaism" or "I was born in America." When you identify yourself with your beliefs, you immediately act defensively against anyone who does not believe the same doctrine as you. Self-identification is misleading because you think your beliefs are you. You are not your conditioning. Learn from your cells.

You are the result of all humankind's conditioning. The whole history of humanity is written inside you. Are you the product of society—or is society a product of you? No matter what time in history, there have always been wars, killing, and violence. Have you ever taken the time to ask why? Why have so many people been killed in the name of God, country, or political beliefs?

I want to analyze the root of violence. Not the name in which the violence is performed, just the violence itself. When you identify yourself as an "American" or a "Christian," a "conservative "or a "liberal," you are being violent. Separation produces violence. When you identify yourself with your conditioning, you think, speak, and act in defense of whatever you believe you are. You protect your limitations and expect unity and peace. Society is the outward reflection of your conditioning. Wars come from projecting the violence you have inside. It is really simple: When there is division, there is conflict. When there is unity, there is peace.

I want to share my personal experience about how my conditioning produced violence in myself and the people around me. Be aware because your conditioning is always going to fight to survive. I was born into a Jewish family in Mexico City. The Jewish community is around sixty thousand people. Just to put this in perspective, there are around twenty million people in the city. The people in the community live in the same neighborhoods, and everybody knows each other. I grew up going to a Jewish school. All my friends from school were Jewish too. They did not force us to go to temple or eat kosher. However, the one thing that was always made clear was that if you were to marry someone, they had to be Jewish. Many people decide to marry a non-Jewish partner and end up not being a part of the community. Living in a close-knit community has its pros and cons, but for the point I am making, I just want to provide my background so we can explore where violence originates.

I was a good basketball player. When I was around thirteen years old, I was selected to play on the national team. I was the only Jewish kid playing on this team. I got along with my teammates. Even to this day, I still talk to some of them. However, the coaching staff always made distinctions. I was always treated differently than the rest, and I never understood why. All I wanted to do was play basketball. It was my life. What does it matter how I was raised or what god I believed in?

A similar experience happened twelve years later. I was living in Los Angeles and was in a relationship with this girl. Our relationship was pure. We were both young, happy, and full of energy. After being together for around six months, my business partners, who were Orthodox Jews, started to give me "advice." Specifically, about what would happen to my children if I were to marry this girl who was not Jewish. They told me endless stories about people who married non-Jewish partners and ended up suffering. My business partners sincerely cared and were giving me advice based on their conditioning. It is funny because I was not even thinking about marriage or having children. I was twenty-six years old!

My then-girlfriend came from a Catholic background. Her parents had many Jewish friends, and they understood how Jewish people only marry each other. When I met them, we spent a lot of the time talking about the difference between my Jewish conditioning and their Catholic one. The energy was always rooted in what makes us different and not in what connects us. Naturally, my relationship with her parents was not great, but who can blame them? Who do you think is more violent? My business partners or my ex-girlfriend's parents? As long as anyone takes an opposing side, it is impossible to meet.

When I started getting free from my conditioning, I finally understood why all of this had happened for me. Being born into the Jewish community, my basketball coach, my business partners, and my ex-girlfriend's parents were all teaching me that, unconsciously, I was still acting under the influence of my conditioning. I began to question who was being violent. Was the violence coming from the coaching staff? Was it coming from the Mexican-Jewish community? Were my business partners being violent advising me? What about the parents of my ex-girlfriend? The answer is everyone! They were all fighting to defend their conditioning. Between two belief systems, there is no real communication and no possibility for harmony. As long as you defend anything, you are being violent. Is it possible to live without conditioning? Without defending? Without being violent? Violence is inside all of us, and we need to see it clearly. If you can be free from your conditioning, you can eliminate the violence in the whole world. It all starts within yourself.

It is pretty clear that the more you believe you are your conditioning, the less you know who you are. You make others wrong to feel a stronger sense of who you think you are. Do you know that if everyone would be an American, no one would? You can only label yourself in comparison to someone else. If everyone was the same height, you could not know whether you are tall or short (more on duality later).

You define yourself in terms of your enemy. All explicit enemies are implicit allies. This contradiction creates conflict. As a Japanese Zen master said, "Don't seek truth—just drop your opinions." No matter what religion you practice or what belief system you are defending, you will always be in conflict as long as you have divisions within yourself. When you defend your conditioning, you are only defending an illusion. In other words, an illusion is defending an illusion. It is impossible to grow and be free while being defensive at the same time. Remember, righteousness is the golden chain. When you stop identifying yourself with all concepts, who are you? Underneath your body, mind, and belief systems, you are one with life itself. Truth behind all is the same. See unity in diversity.

Now, let's take my personal experience and put it in a global context. Throughout history, Jewish people have been persecuted and horrifically killed. The paradox is that the Jewish community still embraces being different. Am I responsible for this violence? I want to take responsibility for all the violence in the world because I know society is a reflection of myself. By identifying myself with my conditioning, I experience violence everywhere.

When I was able to look at the problem of violence without defending any point of view, I stopped producing it. I realized there are no sides. It is just the story you identify yourself with. Because you believe you are that story, you are ready to fight for it. Any identification with your conditioning creates separation and a false sense of self. The self you are trying to defend does not exist. Separation creates violence, and not knowing who you truly are creates violence.

Can you see the contradiction in the way you are living? You say you want peace and harmony, but you work so hard to separate from others. You create disharmony and violence inside and complain about the world being in chaos. How contradictory is this? Obviously, if you want to live in a peaceful world, you first need to find peace internally. Unless there is harmony inside, it cannot exist outside. As long as you see yourself as separate: White, Black, Christian, or Muslim, the violence in the world is never going to stop. What belief is making you feel separate from the rest of humanity? Just look at it, be aware of it, and analyze it for yourself. How is your conditioning influencing your behavior? Just watch!

Now, let's analyze any revolution that has ever happened in this world. It could be Stalin defeating the czars or Fidel Castro overthrowing the Batista government. For any revolutionary to defeat their enemy, they have to become the same or worse as the group they are fighting. When they get power, they start oppressing the other side. Stalin and Castro became tyrants—the very same force they were fighting against. Strange paradox. It is like the state trying to teach people not to murder people by killing people! Violence cannot end violence. The only way that a revolution can actually work is with an expansion of consciousness. Expansion of consciousness brings understanding. Expansion of consciousness eliminates righteousness. When you stop defending the illusion of your conditioning, you begin eliminating the root of violence. Remember the Maharishi effect? When an individual experiences peace within, it alters their surroundings. Individual consciousness creates collective consciousness. It starts with you, every day of your life.

What is the cause of aggression? It is fear, is it not? Religious teachings are belief systems that are part of the mind structure, and fear is inherent in any belief system. When your mind is caught in fear, you live confused and defensive. The moment you identify yourself with something, your intellect only functions to protect it. As long as you wear some identity, you are never going to find peace. When you understand you are not your belief systems, fear disappears. Repeat J. Krishnamurti's insight constantly: "I don't want to have a breath of hate, jealousy, anxiety, or fear in me." To put it simply: no fear, no violence. Evil only comes in the form of unconsciousness. And we all suffer from it because what you do to others, you do to yourself. We will never reach harmony as a human family if we are still defending our separateness.

I am not saying to stop your traditions. I am saying to see your traditions as a method of expression and liberation—not as division and bondage. You do not need to get rid of your conditioning, but you can go beyond it. By beyond, I mean go inside yourself, quiet the mind, and listen. Get to know who you really are: loving awareness. Come back into the very core of your being. As Eckhart Tolle said, "All religions are equally false and equally true, depending on how you use them." Truth cannot be mine or yours. It cannot be Hindu or Jew, American or Russian. Truth is universal. Whenever a set of beliefs claims it is the only truth, it cannot be. It is only the mind projecting it. You are looking at the river reflecting the moon. Whenever there is any disturbance in the river, you think the moon moves.

All you have to do is quiet your mind and look up. When you look up, you wake up!

How can you help anybody if you have not found yourself? It is fundamental that you find yourself first so then you can take care of the rest of the world later. If you are on an airplane and it loses pressure, the emergency procedure is to "put on your mask first and then assist the person next to you." A person in a sandstorm cannot save another. Living from the place of loving awareness is the most you can do for humanity.

Jesus said, "Love your neighbor as you love yourself." But if you do not know who you are, how can you love yourself? You are living in fear, righteousness, and defensiveness, so loving your neighbor becomes impossible. When you find yourself, you love your neighbor automatically because you realize they are a mirror reflecting yourself back at you. Be the mirror of love that you are. When you are awakened, you are not awake as an American or a Jew. You are awake as *being*, and that is universal.

Worship has become more important than love. Instead of seeing all the masters, such as Jesus, Mohammed, Buddha, Krishna, or Moses, as objects of worship, let's see them as examples of humanity. Instead of worshipping them, let's become them. Because I know there is no one more compassionate than you. There is no one more loving than you. Wake up! See your magnificence. Let's create a world where we have religions of joy, politics of love, and humanity of unity. We are one decision away from creating a nonviolent world. But remember, words, labels, and concepts can only take you so far. They allow you to understand, but experience allows you to know. Go beyond yourself by quieting the mind. Silence is how God communicates with you. Silence destroys your conditioning. Silence brings freedom. And with freedom, there is no violence.

AHIMSA (NONVIOLENCE)

THE YAMAS AND THE NIYAMAS ARE THE FIRST TWO LIMBS OF RAJA Yoga. Yamas and Niyamas are ethical preparation to change your attitude about yourself and the rest of the world. Yamas are self-control over your thoughts and actions: nonviolence, truthfulness, non-stealing, non-excess, and non-possessiveness. For example, if you are selfish, untruthful, or greedy, it will be impossible for your mind to be at peace.

Niyamas are used to control your attention. The Niyamas are purity, contentment, self-discipline, self-study, and surrender. Raja Yoga is a scientific way to transcend your mind and experience a state of oneness called *Samadhi*. The goal is for the mind to be at peace because if it is not under control, you cannot transcend it.

Nonviolence is fundamental to all Yogic philosophy. The first Yama in the first limb is *ahimsa*, which means nonviolence. Many people interpret ahimsa as non-killing, yet this is not its totality. Ahimsa is not to cause pain. You can create a lot of suffering through your thoughts, words, and actions. Violence is always created when you lack awareness. For example, I saw a guy saying hateful things to a girl at a party.

Her facial expression and energy collapsed. She started crying and left the party.

I asked the guy, "What happened? Why are you acting this way?"

He defensively answered, "I didn't do anything. She's crazy."

Violence can be expressed in many ways. Always remember that lack of awareness causes pain. Violence is expressed in many forms. If you do not cultivate nonviolence inwardly, it is expressed outwardly. You need to be aware of your thoughts and words for your actions to be impeccable.

Ahimsa starts with bringing balance to your body. Balance brings a state of ease, peace, and harmony. Subsequently, being out of balance brings dis-ease (lack of ease), violence, and disharmony. Self-care is ahimsa. When you eat, move, and sleep well, you bring balance into your life.

Your body is the environment in which you experience life, and you need to take care of it to experience an abundant one. When your body is in balance, you can enjoy life. If you overeat, you lose balance and experience a lack of ease. In Mexico, they call this *mal del puerco* (pig disease). Your body uses all its energy to digest the extra food, and you end up feeling exhausted. When you overeat, you are being violent. Similarly, when you under-sleep, you end up consuming coffee, sugar, or energy drinks to make it through the day. Scientific studies say that when people under-sleep, they eat around four hundred calories more because their bodies need to get the energy from somewhere. When you do not rest, you are being violent. Practicing ahimsa is a daily decision. Creating a peaceful environment in your body is the first step in creating a harmonious life.

As you need to bring balance to your body, you also need to bring it to your mind. Your mind tends to think selfish thoughts when it is in a perspective of fear. Living in fear makes you feel powerless and out of balance. Feeling powerless creates frustration and anger, which manifest in two directions: outward with aggression and intimidation or inward into depression. Outward violence is expressed by being aggressive or intimidated by others. Inward violence is expressed by feeling inadequate or by being too hard on yourself. Shame is a common side effect of being violent toward yourself. Fear is the cause of aggression. If you want to practice ahimsa, you need to transcend fear. When you are dealing with a fearful thought, invite an opposite one. The mind can only think one thought at a time. Try thinking two things at the same time. See, it's impossible! When you notice that your mind is going into a downhill thought pattern, invite an uplifting one. This creates balance. Personally, when I notice that my thoughts are giving me anxiety, I start thinking of my nieces right away, and the environment in my entire body changes. When your mind is in balance, you are living in ahimsa.

How you feel inside yourself is a reflection of how you treat other people. Have you ever noticed when you feel good, confident, and happy, you are more compassionate? On the contrary, when you are tired, hungry, or insecure, any minor disturbance makes you react violently. Practicing nonviolence starts on the inside. Cultivate compassion inside yourself. Refuse to judge yourself over and over for things that already happened. Self-love is the greatest form of nonviolence. Overdoing, overworking, and under-sleeping create a violent inner world that manifests outwardly. How you judge yourself is how you judge people around you. Awareness is the core of nonviolence.

Remember that everyone, including yourself, is doing the best they can with their current level of awareness.

Ahimsa gets tricky with the people you love most. Usually, you think you know what is best for the people you love. You try so hard to take away any form of suffering you believe they may have. Living in nonviolence means trusting that everyone, including your loved ones, will find the answers they seek. A perfect example is when my brother decided to sell his business in Mexico City and move to Miami Beach. He and his wife had two kids at the time.

My mom was naturally worried. She would ask me, "How is he going to provide for his family? Are they going to be happy there? How are my grandkids going to adapt to their new school?" She had many concerns.

The funny thing was when I spoke to my brother, he had zero doubts. He was confident and energized. He knew that moving would be the best decision for him and his family. Everything fell into place, and he became a successful businessman in Miami. You can see my mom's concerns were a waste of energy. My mom believed she was coming from a place of love, but in reality, she was being violent because her worry was really saying that my brother would not figure it out. I always say, "Mom, if you get worried about me, my brother, or my sister, you are insulting us because your worry is a form of not trusting our capacity to deal with whatever circumstance life presents us." Do not confuse love with worry. Worry is a form of violence disguised as caring. It is like the story of a monkey grabbing a fish and saying, "I saved the fish from drowning!" Not knowing he had stopped the fish from living.

Every time you move through adversity, you develop skills and build character. It is in your human nature that you do not want the people you love to suffer. If they have a decision to make, you usually want to tell them how they should act. When you try to take away others' suffering, you think you are being compassionate, but in reality, you are being violent because you are stealing their learning. You are not allowing them to develop confidence.

Taking someone's suffering away does not belong to you. This does not mean you cannot support your loved ones; it means you should not manipulate them and try to control them. It also means that you need to accept that the people you love will pass through adversity. Just as you are blessed when you experience adversity, you should be grateful that the people you love are learning and growing too.

Whenever you give any form of advice, ask yourself, "Does it come from a place of worry or a place of love?" If it comes from a place of worry, you are being violent. If it comes from a place of love, you are practicing ahimsa. Please understand that you do not have any *right* to take anybody's suffering away. What you do have is the *responsibility* to create an environment where they can release their suffering *if* they want to.

By practicing ahimsa, you create a state of balance that manifests in your surroundings. You need to be in balance to live in harmony, but do not think that balance is stagnant. Balance is in motion; true balance is in your ability to let go. For example, if you want to increase the balance in your body by standing on one leg while holding onto a wall, it is not true balance. True balance happens when you let go of the wall. Your conditioning, attachments, and fears act as the wall and keep you stuck in your limited reality. True balance is in motion. True balance is moving with the universe, which is constantly changing. True balance is being nonviolent. As Yoda said, "Train yourself to let go of everything you fear to lose."

The degree to which you are afraid of losing something is in correlation to the degree where you are not free. What would happen if you let go of these fears? Every situation that is presented to you is an opportunity to practice ahimsa. Cultivate seeds of love while trimming the roots of violence. If Gandhi, by practicing ahimsa, defeated the British army without firing a gun, imagine how being nonviolent can change your experience of life.

LIFE IS RELATIONSHIPS

THE WAY YOU EXPERIENCE LIFE IS EXPRESSED IN HOW YOU RELATE to everything around you. Every experience needs relativity. You know yourself in relation to everything else. Think about it, for you to be tall, someone has to be short. If everyone were the same height, no one would be tall or short. How you relate to everything—including your body, money, food, family, and so on—is how you experience the world.

There are areas in your life where your relationships thrive and others where the way you relate has a limited perspective. If you go to work only for a paycheck, this means your relationship to whatever you call work is limited. It has nothing to do with the work itself. This is why people have the same job, and one enjoys it, and the other does not. When you go to a coffee shop, two people are working: one guy makes the coffee and gives it to you with indifference, and the other looks like an artist making coffee with a big smile. The task is the same, but the relationship to what they are doing is entirely different. Enjoyment does not depend on what you do but on your relationship to it. In what areas of your life do you experience happiness and creativity? In what areas do you experience stress and anxiety? As with everything, the way to improve your life always starts with increasing awareness.

So, begin to notice how you feel around different people and situations. Get to know how you relate to the world.

There are four states of consciousness that every human experiences, depending on how they relate to life. The first state is *blame consciousness*. This is when you think that life is happening *to* you. You believe that something outside yourself can determine your happiness. You constantly blame other people and circumstances for your misfortunes. You do not feel in control or responsible for your life. You think that something out there is doing this *to* you. The questions you ask include "Why me?" and "Why does this keep happening?" The blame story is letting you know in what area you have a limited relationship.

The second state is *beneficiary consciousness*; you see that life is happening *for* you. This is when you realize that life is setting you up for success. You know that every situation is working in your favor. If you encounter difficulties in an area that you relate with beneficiary consciousness, you do not react. You calmly respond because you know this situation is tailor-made for you.

The third state is *flow consciousness*: here, you see that life is happening *through* you. In this area, you feel creativity passing through you. You are the channel in which the universe expresses itself. Time seems nonexistent. Ten hours may pass without you even realizing it. In a state of flow, you are not the doer. You are allowing it to happen. The whole is acting through you.

The fourth state is *love consciousness*: here, you feel that life is happening *as* you. You do not feel separate from the rest of the universe. Duality ends. You experience yourself as you truly are: unconditional love. You are in a total state of being. You are one with life and not separate from it. Ask yourself these questions:

- In what areas am I complaining?
- Where do I blame people or circumstances the most?
- In what areas am I the benefactor?
- Where do I feel that everything always seems to work out?
- In what areas do I feel in flow?
- Where do I feel like a channel of creativity?
- In what areas do I feel I am one with life?
- Where do I feel unconditional love?

You can be in love consciousness in your relationship with your spouse. While at the same time, you can be in blame consciousness in relation to your body. Stages are not linear, so be aware.

The main difference between blame and beneficiary consciousness is responsibility. In blame consciousness, you feel like a victim and think that life is unfair. If eating healthy feels like a drag, and each time you eat a dessert, you blame yourself; this is where you need to shift your relationship from blame to beneficiary consciousness. To transcend to a beneficiary state, you need to realize that the only way you can have a powerful life is by acknowledging that you are fully responsible. Responsibility is your ability to respond to whatever happens to you. When you assume complete accountability for everything life throws at you, you understand the power of your inner being. When you become 100 percent responsible, nothing you experience feels unfair. When you change your contact lenses from blame to beneficiary, you automatically alter your relationship to life. You stop being a victim of circumstances and control and begin to experience surrender and trust. You stop imagining worst-case scenarios and start putting your attention on best-case scenarios. In blame consciousness, you are reacting; in beneficiary consciousness, you are responding. In other words, reactivity is bondage; responsibility is freedom.

In beneficiary consciousness, you begin pursuing your desires, yet there is still a feeling of separateness because your desires are limited by your perspective. Your mind is limited to what it can imagine. When you look at life through the lens of a benefactor, you naturally start taking more risks because you understand everything will work out for you. Even if you fail, you will end up learning. Failure is good luck in disguise. Failure is only teaching you what you need to learn to expand your perspective. You place less importance on the outcome and more on the learning.

The difference between beneficiary and flow consciousness is the power of surrender. In flow consciousness, you work as the channel. You have unlimited potentiality. In other words, "by me, limited by my own perspective; through me, unlimited by the universe."

Psychologist Mihaly Csikszentmihalyi explains flow as "a state in which people are so involved in an activity that nothing else seems to matter." People experiencing flow create remarkable results. When Kobe Bryant scored a career-high eighty-one points, he described that he got into a state of flow that felt like an out-of-body experience. In flow consciousness, ideas come through you. If you do not express them, someone else will. Michael Jackson understood this principle really well. He used to call his manager at three o'clock in the morning to tell him an idea that he wanted to express on stage.

The manager replied, "It's three a.m. we will talk about it tomorrow."

But Michael insisted, "We have to write it down right now because if we do not, Prince will."

In love consciousness, the universe manifests as you in the form of bliss. When you are in bliss, you automatically activate your full potential. Bliss is the experience when the universe gets to know itself. The universe is alive in you. When you are in love with someone, you can feel that you and your significant other at moments are one. At this moment, life is happening *as* you. You are an expression of love itself. You do not want to accomplish or get anything from anyone because you realize how perfect and complete life is. The same experience happens when you eat your favorite food. At that moment, you do not want to be somewhere else. You do not chase or pursue because there is no lack in you. You are in a state of bliss. You are your true self: unconditional love.

In essence, this is how is goes: First, you go from blaming life, being defensive, and being controlling to appreciating life and pursuing your goals and inspirations. After that, you realize something you cannot even dream of is happening *through* you. Finally, you recognize that there is nothing to accomplish. This moment is absolutely perfect. You are here as a mirror of love and compassion for everyone else. You live in a state of bliss because you are unconditional love.

You cannot change your circumstances instantly, but you can change your relationship with them. The only thing you can change immediately is your attitude. You have the power of perception—not what you perceive. There is where your responsibility lies. People love to make excuses and blame circumstances for preventing their evolution. For example, if you are a mother, you may believe that you do not have time for your own growth practices. You say things like, "I would mediate if I did not have to drop off my kids at school" or "I would exercise if I had more time."

You need to understand that your kids are your yoga. Learn how to grow from where you are. The situation you are going through is the one you need to wake up. This is Karma Yoga. You can use anything as an instrument for growth. You can turn any activity into meditation. After all, what is meditation? It is focusing your full attention on what you are doing. You can be a kindergarten teacher and experience a state of flow. Remember, it is not what you do; it is how you do it. When you take a bath, take it totally. When you are eating, eat. If you are watching a movie, watch the movie. Do not browse your phone or get distracted by a million and one things. When you focus your complete attention on what you are doing, there is no room for your imaginary problems. This is the optimal experience. Remember, stress exists only if you create it.

You have experienced the state of being that is ultimately love consciousness. This state feels like you are one with the universe. It can be when you surf a wave, and everything aligns itself perfectly. It could be when you are cooking, and after you finish, you taste it—and it is exactly how you imagined it would be. It could be the moment you buy a new car, and when you are driving it, you lose track of time and experience a blissful feeling. The problem comes when you confuse any activity with a state of being. Instead of focusing on being unconditional love, you end up chasing waves, cooking, or working your ass off to buy a new car.

Now, let's analyze the most important relationship you have in life: your relationship with the present moment. If you treat the present as a means to an end, you will always be busy trying to get somewhere else. If you see the present as not good enough, it is a sign of blame consciousness. The future is infinite possibilities, but if you treat the present as a means to an end, your future is no longer a future—and your present is no longer a present. Every time you complain, you are relating to the present moment as if it were your opponent.

Your relationship to time is fundamental for experiencing love consciousness. In the present is the field of infinite possibilities. In the mind is the field of stress and anxiety. Stress and anxiety cut off the connection of creativity from the universe to you. You enjoy any activity in which you are truly present. Get rid of the illusion that the circumstances are somehow imperfect.

If you protest anything that happens, you are automatically blocking your own power. When you are responsible for everything that happens, you get access to the power of now. The purpose of life is not in the future, but if you are going to look for it there, you will be looking on and on and on.

The cycle of any experience goes like this: How you relate to (fill in the blank) creates your perception. Your perception creates your belief system. Your belief system creates your behavior, and your behavior is based on how you relate to the world. This always happens cyclically. Are you responsible for how people relate to you? People respond based on your response, and you respond based on theirs. This is the cycle.

I have a friend who was having problems relating to her mother-in-law. For almost a year, every time they had to spend time together, it was always a drag. When we started working with her consciousness, she shifted her lens from blame to beneficiary. Instead of seeing her mother-in-law as the reason she was feeling inner disturbance, she saw her mother-in-law as the vehicle who revealed a limited belief inside herself.

A funny thing happened. She changed her perspective, and the next day, her mother-in-law texted her with a completely different attitude. If you change your perspective, that is to say, who you are in relation to whoever you are looking at; you alter the way you perceive the world and how the world perceives you.

Wayne Dyer said, "If you change the way you look at things, the things you look at change." Relationships are the mirror in which you get to know yourself. The purpose of relationships is to choose what part of you you would like to experience. And remember that there are no obligations in any relationships; there are only opportunities.

The foundation of abundance is to focus on the things that are working for you. If you focus on what you lack—money, love, or relationships—you will always feel insufficient no matter the amount of money, friends, or girlfriends you may have. If you do not change the way you relate to your limitations, you will always bring them with you no matter what you experience. You keep the limitations you try to defend. Instead of trying to change the world, better, change the relationship you have with it. The way you talk to yourself shapes the lens through which you perceive the world. If you try to change the world before you change the concept you have of yourself, it is like buying groceries with

Monopoly money. In other words, absurd. The only thing you need to change is the concept you have of yourself and how you relate to life because life is relationships.

A key lesson I learned in my yoga teacher training was that it is more important to have flexibility in the mind than flexibility in the body. If you are not flexible in the mind, you will constantly be fighting because no adjustments are available. If your mind is flexible, adjustments happen naturally—and life becomes easy. Flexibility in the mind means you understand that if you experience suffering, it is because of how attached you are to your perspective.

Flexibility in the mind means you are fully responsible for your inner being. Imagine a scale of blaming versus loving. On this scale, you see areas of your life that seem unfair, others that seem fun, and some that feel like a roller coaster of creativity. The purpose of anything you do is to experience who you truly are: unconditional love. Do not confuse any activity with a state of being. Stop looking for something to do—and start looking for something to *be*. Do not rely on your work for realization. Give all the magic abundantly that lives inside you, and everything that resides outside will be attracted to you automatically. Ask yourself, "What am I am *being* when I feel joyful?" Change your relationship with time; instead of measuring your days by productivity, measure them by your state of being. Did you feel fulfilled and loving today? You are pursuing something that you already possess. Your life is defined by the state of consciousness in which you live. Remember, it is never about somebody or something else. It is always about your relationship with it.

YOUR WORRY IS BLOCKING
YOUR POTENTIAL

HAVE YOU EVER NOTICED THAT PEOPLE WHO TEND TO WORRY END up worrying about everything? It does not matter what happens—worry is their reality. When they overcome their worry, another one immediately pops up. If you think about it, there is always something you could worry about—money, health, politics, the weather, the Lakers—the number of things are infinite.

Worry is a chronic condition that has no end. We all know someone who worries about everything, like if it is going to rain or if there is going to be traffic. Even if there is no traffic, they say, "What's wrong? Why is there no traffic?" Whenever you are anxious and imagining worst-case scenarios, you train your mind how to respond. Why do you always tend to imagine what could go wrong? Do not practice what you do not want to become. It's funny how nowadays people are learning stress management. Why would you want to learn how to manage something you do not like? Learn how to manage your body, business, and your relationships—not your stress! Stress never happens because something happens. It only happens because you do not know how to handle your mind.

Worry is like an infinite onion. You peel the onion, and

the more it reduces in size, your line of vision changes. You are constantly peeling and peeling, however the onion always appears the same size. Whenever you peel an onion, tears come out of your eyes. Similarly, whenever you worry, your cells start crying. Anxiety has an impact on your whole system. If you tend to worry, you do not allow your cells to regenerate. Worrying, anxiety, and stress are the byproduct of most diseases.

Constantly being in a state of stress manifests itself physically, emotionally, and mentally. Worrying is like seeing the onion through a microscope. No matter the size, you are always going to perceive it as a big threat. A potential threat that has not yet happened is self-generated. Being vigilant is based on fear. It is important to realize you are not scared about the future. You are only afraid of your prediction about the future. And your prediction is just in your imagination. There is no future; there is only your internal dialogue about it. Worrying about things that have not yet happened is self-imposed suffering. You are not here to suffer. You do not help anybody by being miserable.

When you look at life through a lens of worry, you tend to imagine worst-case scenarios. The paradox is that by worrying, you are experiencing the event you are trying to avoid. Emotionally, physically, and mentally, you are living a future that has not yet happened. The only thing that is upsetting you is your imagination. That's madness! Imagination is a form of thinking. And what is thinking after all? A voice in your mind talking nonsense. Imagination is making up things that do not exist. If you are going to make up something, at least make up something that makes you joyful.

Worry is mental pain. Do you think that by worrying, you

will take care of your problems? If you do, by all means, worry for three straight weeks. Do not even go to sleep—keep worrying! Worrying is an entirely hopeless pursuit. Worrying is exactly like the *cobra effect*. The cobra effect is when an attempted solution makes a problem worse. When the British government ruled India, they had an overpopulation of cobras. They announced that any citizen who captured a cobra and turned it in would be financially rewarded. What actually happened was that people started breeding cobras to make a profit. This caused the cobra population to skyrocket.

Similarly, when you worry, you are applying the cobra effect to your life. It makes you reactive instead of responsive. As they say, "Worry is the interest paid in advance on a debt you may never owe." When you worry, you think you are worrying about what could happen. But in in reality, you are just worrying about what you're worrying about. Stop this nonsense worrying about worrying.

People tend to confuse worry with responsibility. They feel guilty if they do not worry about things. For example, if you are a mother and do not worry about your kids, you feel like you are a bad mom. If you do not worry about your business, you feel like you are a bad boss. Remember what I tell my mom when she starts worrying: "Mom, if you get worried ... your worry is a form of not trusting our capacity to deal with whatever circumstance life presents us." When you worry, you are not trusting yourself to deal with whatever you will experience.

Do not confuse worry with caring or responsibility. The two most useless emotions are guilt and worry. Guilt has the same energy as worry, but it is about something that already happened.

Do you think that carrying guilt will change the past? If you do, by all means, live in guilt for three straight weeks. Do not even sleep—stay guilty!

Guilt makes you experience an event over and over again, which makes you suffer. That's madness! Learn your lesson and move on. Guilt is always about the past, and worry is always about the future. Both are useless. You only suffer because you do not know how to handle two faculties of your mind: memory and imagination. Your memory makes you suffer for something that already happened. Your imagination makes you suffer over things that have not yet happened. Depression is a past tense emotion, and anxiety is a future one.

The most powerful way to live an abundant life is by trusting yourself, the people around you, and the unseen forces that collaborate with everyone. When you try to control every single outcome, you feel separate from the rest of existence. The only way to become one with the universe is to trust it.

Making decisions creates stress because you try to analyze and collect all the data you can. If you really think about it, there is an infinite amount of data in any decision you make. Anxiety only reinforces the illusion of control. When you worry, you think you can predict variables beyond your control. But who do you think you are to worry? Please send me a text when are worrying because I did not get the memo that you are in charge of the entire cosmos. You do not know enough to worry about anything! You can spend your whole life worrying, and it would not change a thing. The more you let go, the more you trust, the more you enjoy. Accessing your full intelligence, not only your rationality, allows you to make intuitive decisions. Intuitive decisions do not create any stress. Instead of trying to control everything around you, control your reaction to everything around you. If you are smart, you will not waste time worrying about what is unpredictable anyway.

When you practice yoga or any type of movement that challenges your body, your mind tends only to be aware of whatever is uncomfortable. In a yoga class, I was standing on one leg and twisting my body in an advanced position. I thought, *Resist the urge to worry.* Immediately I felt more comfortable and balanced, which allowed me to stay in that position longer. I am also right-handed, so naturally, I am stronger on that side. But instead of calling my left side my weak side, I call it my fun side. It makes the struggle enjoyable. When you reframe something in your mind, it changes your entire body. How cool is that? I have applied these two principles ever since, not just physically but also in every area of my life. When I am in a stressful situation, I say to myself, *Resist the urge to worry.* This allows me to witness my mind. This separation eliminates my worry because I understand that if I can see it, it is not me. The only thing that is worrying is my mind and ego. When I am going to do a project, activity, or anything that is not aligned with my natural skills, I immediately call it the fun (fill in the blank). This allows me to come back to my Shoshin mindset. The struggle always ends up being the most fun I have. So, the next time you experience anxiety, tell yourself to resist the urge to worry. The next time you do something outside your comfort zone, know that it is your fun side of life.

When you put your attention and focus on what can go wrong, you are automatically betting against yourself. How much energy have you spent peeling this infinite onion? Who would you become in the absence of all your worries? Remember, what you focus on grows. When you operate in a state of anxiety, you are literally blocking the flow of energy into your life. When you focus on what can go wrong, you miss the chance to see the hidden opportunities that are presented.

Your worry is blocking your potential! Worry is only an indication of compulsive thinking. Compulsive thoughts do not allow you to access a world of creativity. If you are going to utilize your imagination, use it to imagine the version of yourself you would like to experience. Be in a state that all your dreams have already come true. Know that in everything you have ever done, you were doing the best you could with the level of awareness you had at the time. So, what can you do? The best thing you can do for yourself and others is to raise your level of awareness. Do not make any assumptions about how your path will go. When your mind starts playing tricks, do not be fooled by worry or guilt. Remember, you are spinning around in a sphere that is in the middle of absolutely nowhere. You came here to experience this beautiful reality for some years, so why waste it by being stressed out?

WHY WOULD YOU CHOOSE
MISERY IF JOY IS AVAILABLE?

THE MOST FUNDAMENTAL MISUNDERSTANDING THAT WE HAVE AS a culture is that you believe that the outside world generates your life's experience. Your brain acts as a filter through which you experience the world. The brain processes vibrational information electrically, allowing you to experience sight, sound, taste, smell, and touch.

Everything you perceive is a vibration. The brain decodifies information from the outside world, processes it as an electromagnetic signal, and makes it into a holographic reality. Where do you see this book? You think you see it in front of you, but in fact, you see it inside of you. What is happening is that light is reflecting energy, which your brain decodifies and creates an image. This is why if you turn off the lights, you will not be able to see it. The book is still there, but your brain cannot decodify the information because there is no light.

Everything you experience happens inside yourself. When you taste your favorite meal, you do not taste it with the tongue. You taste it via the tongue. The tongue sends information to your brain, where it decodifies it, and based on your sense of taste, you experience it as tasty or not. When you touch your spouse's hand, you think you are feeling their hand, but in reality, you are feeling the nerves in your hand. Your hand sends information to your brain, and that is why you can feel your hand through your spouse. Your senses give you the impression that what you are experiencing is the outside world. But, in reality, every experience always comes from within. Scientists have known this for a while. In hospitals, they use a system that stops the information that travels from the point of pain to the brain. If the brain cannot decodify the message, you cannot feel pain. What you are aware of is just vibrations passing through your nervous system. So, where do you experience the world? Inside yourself! The world is in you—not you in the world.

Experiences of pain and pleasure are not from the outside. They are only interpretations of your mind. No matter what you are experiencing—joy or misery, happiness or anger, agony or bliss—it all comes from within. Your internal perception shapes the way you see the world. If you are angry, you are wearing the glasses of anger, which makes you experience an angry reality. If you are sad, your glasses of perception make you experience sadness in whatever you do. If you are joyful, no matter if someone cuts you off in traffic or you miss the subway, you still experience joy.

Senses can give you chaotic information if you do not sharpen them. The world is your projection, and the projection is the film of life through your mind. According to the filter you look through, you experience the world. If you are a thief, you naturally distrust everybody. It is your mental attitude that determines what you see. Look at a paranoid person. He experiences an anxious and threatened reality. The paranoia came from some past experience, but he kept the filter. The filter is the one that decodifies the information in his brain and makes him experience a distorted reality. Joy and misery do not depend on outside events; they depend on how you interpret them. If you learn how to control your inner experience, you can determine the quality of your life. Understand you are experiencing life not because life is the way it is; but because you are the way you are! Different experiences happen based on how you digest the world passing through you. Life provides the stimulus; you provide the reaction.

If every experience comes from within, why are people stressed and anxious? The only thing that is happening call it depression, stress, or PTSD, is that people do not know how to handle their intelligence. Learning how to manage your thoughts and emotions is learning how to use your full intelligence. No inner order means inner chaos. A lack of inner order manifests as stress and anxiety. Outside events appear purely as information— without a positive or negative value attached.

Your interpretation determines how you experience an event. You tend to use outside stimuli to generate inner order. This makes you a slave to circumstances. Changing external conditions only works momentarily. If you buy a new car, you experience pleasure until you do not. Then you try to pursue the next event or possession. When you do not learn how to manage your intelligence, no matter what happens, you always experience disharmony. Knowing how to handle your intelligence means you can experience anything that happens as joy. If you are miserable, and you achieve or purchase something, will you enjoy it? But if you are joyful, and you do not achieve or buy anything, do you care? If you know how to handle your thoughts, emotions, energy, and chemistry, you can experience joy as a default setting. The only thing you need to learn is how to manage the energies within you. If you are in harmony, you always find meaning in what you are experiencing—no matter what is happening. You, and you alone, cause your experience of life. You claim your power when outside events do not dictate your inner experience. If you learn how to handle your inner order, who or what can enslave you? You can create your own experience. If you can create your own experience, which one would you rather have: joy or misery?

When you do not have an external stimulus, your attention wanders, and that is when you experience anxiety. If you do not know how to control your attention, your attention is naturally drawn to the first worry that crosses your mind. As soon as your mind is ready to relax, there it is again. The potential problem you imagine returns. For this reason, people spend most of their time watching Netflix marathons or browsing social media. Television and social media give accessible information that organizes your attention. When you have a breakup, or you are bored, you turn on the TV. Although it creates an order of attention, this does not mean it brings a positive experience. You are momentarily bringing order to your consciousness, but you are not learning how to control your inner experience. As soon as you turn off the TV, the lack of inner order returns—and you look for another distraction.

Until you learn how to focus your attention, your mind will keep creating all kinds of troubles. All actions make impressions in your mind. It is up to you to make the proper impressions. What can possibly be wrong with this moment? Only what you imagine it is. Every cell in your body, through your senses, is receiving feedback from life. But who is doing the filtering? Your conditioning? Your memory? Your insecurities? Anxieties? Your inner conflict comes because of your filtering. You live carrying the filters of expectations, goals, and desires. That is why you experience reality as you think it is—and not as it really is. The human brain contains one hundred billion cells, which is the same number of stars in the universe. Realize that there is nothing wrong with the world. The only thing that is happening is something inside you is not functioning in harmony. Learn how to use your full intelligence. Remember you are not afraid of the future; you are only afraid of your *idea* about it.

Every experience you can possibly have always comes from inside yourself. There is nothing wrong with the world—only the way you look at it. When you change your perspective, you change your reality. Your reality is based on your thoughts and mental attitude. If you remember that, you do not put so much stress on outside events.

Please understand that events, people, and circumstances cannot make you suffer or give you joy. Only your attitude toward them does that. Focus on controlling your inner state instead of your outer environment. As Neale Donald Walsch said, "Until you decide what something means, it does not have any meaning at all."

If someone else could decide your inner experience, would this not be the ultimate slavery? Viktor Frankl, a psychologist and Holocaust survivor, said, "Everything can be taken from a man but one thing: the last of the human freedoms—to choose one's attitude in any given set of circumstances."

Even in extreme conditions, you still have the ability to choose how you are going to respond. You are the source of your reality. Wherever you go, you carry a sense of awareness that lets you know you are here and now. This means that time and space are in you—not the other way around. You are not in your body; the body is not the experiencer. You experience life by the mind and through the body. Your body and mind are only a vehicle. This means that the body and mind are in you—not the other way around. You are the witness behind them. All the universe is in you and cannot be without you. Without you, where is the world? Without the perceiver, where is the perceived? The world is because you are. Nothing exists separate from you. When you realize this, you wake up from the dream. You are free.

Heaven and hell are imagined as geographical places. Heaven is described as a place in the clouds where people live in mansions with all of their loved ones. In heaven, there is no violence, and there is always a big party going on. Everyone is always happy, dancing, singing, and celebrating. Hell is imagined as being at the bottom of the earth, where everything is hot. It's a place of punishment where people suffer.

Now, let's think that through. Heaven and hell are described, at least in the biblical sense, as being in time and space. This means that you are in heaven and hell right now! How would you describe your experience when you are jealous? Or when you are angry? You feel like there is a fire burning throughout your body. You think you are being punished, and you suffer. You are in hell at that moment. Hell is a place of fear, anger, violence, judgment, and suffering. You open the gates of hell by your lust, greed, and lack of compassion. If there is hell in your mind, it is going to be impossible for you to experience heaven—even if you are in the middle of it!

How would you describe your experience when you are in love or when you are creative? You feel so light, as if you could fly. You feel ecstatic, grateful, and connected to the rest of existence. You are experiencing heaven on earth. Heaven and hell are not geographical places. They are only what you make of yourself. Heaven and hell only exist in the mind. Hell is simply disharmony within you. It is your expectations that are creating your hell. Your suffering is based on your models of how you think the universe should be, which creates resistance. In other words, resistance is living in hell. Remember, heaven is always here. It is never there. It is always now. It is never then. Heaven is always inside your heart. How you feel within yourself determines the quality of your life. Hell is the feeling of separateness. Heaven is the feeling of unity. The world is not projected onto you. It is created by you. Make your world perfect—and see it as play. If you learn how to use your full intelligence, heaven is going to be your reality.

People tend to describe divinity by human standards, which is absolute nonsense. They live in fear, trying to go to heaven and avoiding hell. Once you place God and the devil as opposites, they become equals. Hell creates a mockery out of free will. Imagine if I take my niece into a candy store and say, "Sweetie, you can pick whatever you want. I love you no matter what."

She goes around and picks out some chocolate.

When I see the chocolate, I say, "Why would you pick

chocolate? What's wrong with you? I am going to send you to hell forever and ever."

Of course, she would respond, "You told me I could pick whatever I wanted. Why are you punishing me?"

Similarly, they say that God loves you no matter what, but if you pray to another one, you will go to hell. This is not a loving God, is it? It is a jealous one. Jealousy is a human condition, not a divine one. It is fundamental to realize that heaven and hell do not exist in another plane. They exist right now. You create hell when you are not compassionate, when you are greedy, and when you act unconsciously. You create hell when you forget who you really are.

The greatest evil in the world is ignorance. The greatest virtue is wisdom. Wisdom is not intellectual knowledge. Wisdom is knowing who you really are: an individualization of divinity. Believing in heaven and hell takes away your responsibility because your actions are always based on fear. You defer your responsibility to an imaginary authority that judges you by human standards. How liberated would you feel in the absence of the idea of hell? And how magnificent it is to realize you are in heaven right now! Ignorance creates hell. Wisdom creates heaven. Do not polish your ignorance. Get rid of it so you can remember who you really are.

Everything you experience is just your brain decodifying information. You can interpret the information the outside world is supplying as a possibility or as a problem. The only thing you need to learn is how to manage your attention. You can enjoy all situations if you develop the ability to focus on the present moment. If you learn how to manage your body, energy, and emotions, who cares what happens outside?

Right now, you are like a ping-pong ball, bouncing from situation to situation, experiencing the world based on what life throws at you. When you learn how to create a stable platform to generate inner order, you become the ping-pong player instead of the ball. Do not forget that every possible human experience is always generated from within. The human brain is magnificent. It is what allows you to experience the ecstasy of being alive. Just learn how to use it. An airplane is an amazing tool, but if you do not know how to fly it, it can kill you. Once you master yourself, you live in heaven over hell. Because why would you choose misery if joy is available?

THE PHYSICS OF SPIRITUALITY

You experience life through your five senses. You believe that whatever you can see, feel, hear, taste, or touch is all that is real. In reality, many things exist that you cannot perceive. There are radio waves all around you. If you turn on the radio in any part of the world, it picks up a signal, and you can hear whatever the other side is transmitting. Wi-Fi works the same way; it uses radio frequencies to send signals between devices.

There are many electromagnetic waves that you use in day-to-day life without even noticing. If you were to break a bone and go to the doctor, the hospital uses an x-ray device that allows you to see your bones. You cannot see x-rays because they vibrate at a faster frequency than visible light. Just because you cannot perceive them does not mean they are not there.

Ultraviolet light is invisible to the human eye, yet bumblebees can see it. Worms can only perceive sound and touch, so in their reality, everything you see is nonexistent. The universe experiences itself through the nervous system that is looking at it. This is why bumblebees and worms experience different realities than humans. The human nervous system has evolved to experience the universe through the five senses. That is why I have never heard anyone say, "Look, that radio wave is so beautiful" or "I do not like that ultraviolet light in my room." You can only perceive a small part of what is happening in space. Matter is the slowest frequency of information traveling in the universe. This is why you can perceive solid objects. Quantum physics reveals that the space between stuff is not actually empty. Space on the quantum scale is full of energy. There is a field of energy that unifies everything in the universe. This is the quantum field. Once you transcend your senses, you can use your inner technology to experience the whole universe.

The quantum universe was discovered by studying what makes up matter. Let's see how the human body comes into existence. It all begins at the subatomic level. When two atoms bond together, they form a molecule. When molecules bond, it creates a chemical. When chemicals are put together, they form a cell. When cells group together, they form a tissue. When tissue is developed, it creates an organ. Organs together form systems. And all the systems together form a body. In other words, all things, including yourself, are made of atoms. If you peel an atom like you peel an onion, you find a nucleus and subatomic particles like protons, neutrons, and electrons. But for the most part, the atom appears to be 99.99 percent empty (the exact number is 99.999999999999—that's twelve nines!). Before the discovery of quantum physics, it was believed the space inside atoms, just as the space between everything else, was empty. But this space is actually full of energy that carries information. The atoms that create the material world are made out of invisible energy and not tangible matter. This means that atomically, your physical body is mostly made out of energy. How cool is that? You are made out of nothing, yet here you are! Matter is really an illusion. Everything in the universe is energy vibrating in different densities.

Quantum physics studies the things that happen on the smallest scale that underwrite the physical world. On the material level, you can perceive separation. This is why you see objects separate from yourself. Once you look at the world from the inside, you see that there is less separation between molecules on a molecular level. If you go even further, on the atomic level, atoms appear to be even less separate. On the nuclear level, there is even less separation. At the bottom of everything, there is a field of energy that connects us all. There is no separation between you and everything else. Everything in the universe is connected through a field of energy. Each of your cells is sending and receiving information with this field.

When atoms bond, they share information and energy in a particular frequency. Your body contains around thirty-seven trillion cells and seven billion billion billion atoms (that's a 7 followed by 27 zeros!) Scientists have found that the quantum field acts like a hologram. In a hologram, every point contains all the information of the whole. This means that every cell in your body contains the information of the whole universe. If you learn how to access this information, you can access all the secrets of the universe. Enlightened beings figured this out a long time ago, like when Rumi said, "Don't feel lonely, the entire universe is inside of you." This is not a philosophical teaching; this is quantum physics.

How cool is it to know that you are made of the same "stuff" the universe is made of? The answer has always been inside you. There is scientific evidence that at the core, we are all one! Throughout history, this field of energy has been called by many names: scientists call it the unified field, the Hindus call it Brahma, the yogis call it cosmic consciousness, Einstein called it quanta, the Greeks called it Ether, and others call it God. Religious scriptures define God as omnipresent, meaning there is no place where God is not. Similarly, this field of energy is the container of the universe. Nothing can exist outside of it. This field is intelligent and conscious. It is beyond space and time.

You are not a human experiencing the universe. You are the universe experiencing itself through a human. And every other being is too. This is why Ram Dass said, "Treat everyone you meet like God in drag." Because we all are. Nietzsche said that God is dead—that only what you can perceive exists—but he was 100 percent wrong. Matter is dead. Matter is the illusion, not God. Quantum physics proves that all there is is God. An omnipresent field of energy that connects us all.

Nassim Haramein, one of the leading physicists in quantum field theory, explains that the constant exchange of information between you and the field functions in a *feedforward feedback structure*. This means that you are giving information to the field, and the field is sending information to you in return. Each person gives a unique set of information.

Every thought and every emotional response is a frequency. You are the central point of reference of your experience. This means that everything is the center of everything else. You are the universe expressing itself from your central point of vision. For example, if we were sitting at a round table, and I put an object in the middle, each of us would see the object differently. If you change where you are sitting, you change how you see the object.

In other words, if you change your perspective, you are going to send and receive different sets of information.

Cells exchange information via emotions. This is why positive thinking alone is ineffective because it does not create a strong enough signal. Thought plus emotion creates a clear signal. Uplifting emotions like love, joy, and gratitude vibrate faster than downgraded emotions like fear, anxiety, and shame. Remember, matter is the slowest form of vibration, and you need to keep giving the same signal to create the reality you want. Changing signals is like giving your Uber driver different directions. Also, it takes time for your Uber to get you to where you want to go—just like your vibration takes time to materialize. Wherever your awareness goes, matter follows. Life matches whatever information you send. The opinion you have of yourself determines the expression of your life. Fear and anxiety bind you to your present level of consciousness. If I see myself as someone unworthy, I'm emitting that signal, and the universe has no choice but to match that. Life makes no mistakes and gives that which you believe yourself to be. To become the broadest version of yourself, get out of your own way. Focus on possibilities rather than on obstacles and limitations. Abandon your excuses. Take advantage of all the available energy that is at your disposal.

Growth is not linear. Do not live by the misconception that if you make ten dollars this year, the next you will make eleven, and by the time you are sixty-five, you will make a hundred. A quantum jump is when you use the field of infinite possibilities to grow exponentially instead of systematically.

There are two signs that you are in tune with the quantum

leap: *intuition* and *passion*. Intuition is making a decision with the intelligence of your full consciousness. Passion is when you release all the energy you have available in the activity you are doing. Passion and intuition express who you are. Neither signal is ever motivated by fear. In the quantum world, everything already exists—from your biggest nightmare to a life you cannot even dream of and everything in between. A quantum jump is only to become aware of what already exists; reality changes by the very act of observation. Your dream is waiting for you to claim it in order for you to experience it. The universe constantly opens growth opportunities. The consciousness of lack produces scarcity, and life has no other choice but to match it. An abundant universe exists within you. Claim it! Stop living by your limitations and start living by your possibilities. Quantum physics has proven scientifically what karma is. Everything that comes to you is a return of what comes out from you. Do not believe in gradual steps. Take the quantum jump!

There is nothing but energy everywhere. The limits you perceive are just mental boundaries. Consciousness is the source of creation. You and consciousness are one. Absolutely everything you can think of is possible. Attention is the secret of creation, and doubt is always based on a limited perspective. If you are going to doubt something, doubt your rational mind and trust your intuition.

When you start dancing with the field of infinite possibilities, the world begins to behave differently. Your dream starts to move in your direction. Take away your attention from limitations and put it in your imagination. That is why Walt Disney said, "Worry is a waste of imagination." Your state of awareness influences reality. By quantum law, you cannot *become* successful. You can only *be* successful. If you are trying to become successful, it means that you do not *feel* like you already are. The information you are sending is coming from a place of lack. Do not say "I want to be successful." Instead, say, "I have success." Remember, the frequency of wanting and having are different. As long as you make something as an object of wanting, you define yourself as lacking it. A person who is looking for peace is obviously in conflict. Why would you feel scarcity if you already are a seven billion billion billionaire? Just look at the amazing being you already are in a material world made out of nothing. Act as if your dreams have already come true. Act like success in every area of your life is guaranteed. Do not be anxious as far as results. They will come as the sun follows the moon. Remember the physics of spirituality: Life has no choice but to send abundance in every aspect of your life if you *feel* that you already have it ... because you do.

THE FABRIC OF LIFE
IS PURE JOY

THE UNIVERSE IS LIKE THE DILEMMA OF THE ZEBRA. IS A ZEBRA A white horse with black stripes or a black horse with white stripes? Everything that exists in this physical dimension has a dualistic nature. Black implies white, male implies female, right implies wrong, pain implies pleasure, day implies night, self implies others, and life implies death. One cannot buy without a seller or sell without a buyer. Nothing can exist without its opposite. That is why you have never seen a one-sided coin or person with two fronts and no backs. This is the unity of opposites; duality is unity.

When you realize that others cannot exist without you, that you did not arrive here by mistake, you can experience yourself as you really are. In *Vedanta philosophy*, God is not a guy with a white beard, who sits on a throne, carries a spear, and plays chess with human lives in the clouds. God is pure consciousness. Pure consciousness is described in the scriptures as quantum physics describes the quantum field. In this idea, God, like the quantum field, is omnipresent. This means nothing can exist outside of it, and it is in every part of creation. Pure consciousness is not separate from you. God is inside you. Everyone is God in disguise, coming to this dualistic plane to experience themselves because any experience needs relativity.

To put it simply:

- Who am I? The universe expressing itself through a human nervous system.
- Why am I here? To create and experience who I am.

Let's think it through. If you were the creator of the universe, what would you do? Would you sit there in bliss forever and ever and ever? I know I wouldn't. As a creator, you would start to play games. You would get involved in all kinds of adventures. But you would have to forget who you truly are to be entertained. It is like in the middle of a good movie, a great actor would make you forget he is playing a role and you are just watching a film. Similarly, you play your role so well that you forgot who you truly are.

The yogis see the world as drama. The purpose of the universe is the play, the Lila, the dream, the drama of life. Duality is the cosmic show. God is playing hide-and-seek with itself because that is all there is. You forget who you are to find yourself. Stephen Hawking asks, "Why does the universe go to all the bother of existing?" The universe exists because it is the only way it can know itself experientially. The purpose of the play is for the universe to know itself through you. Nisargadatta Maharaj, an enlightened being, said, "Ultimately, you are the proof that God exists, not the other way around. For before any question about God can be put, you must be there to put it."

The divine play of life is often compared to a dream. This is why the process of knowing your true self is called awakening.

You go from being human, the created, and evolve to God, the creator. In other words, you go from *individual consciousness* to *cosmic consciousness*. There is no difference between you and God. And when the play is over, you realize this was all a dream—and we are all one.

How do you know you exist? You have a sense of awareness that is always watching the play of your life. This awareness is how you know you are alive. A sense of knowing that *I Am* separate from knowing *who I Am*. This is why you say, "I am" first and then add "a man," "a woman," "an American," or "a Christian."

Personality comes from the Latin root *persona*, which means *mask*. The mask you use to try to earn love and respect prevents you from knowing you already have it. Strange paradox. You wear many different layers, yet beneath them all, you are the witness, the sense of I AM, watching everything that happens. What you are deep down, the very core of your being, is the fabric of existence itself. You are made of the same stuff the universe is made of. You are all there is; you are God in disguise. Underneath the material world, beneath the physical appearances and separate forms, you are one with all. Each being is a unique way in which the universe experiences itself. Remember how Nassim Haramein describes the quantum field? Inside every atom of creation, there is a field of energy connecting us all. The source of creation is within you. Pretty cool, isn't it?

There are two mantras in the East that have been used for centuries: *So-Ham* and *Sat Chit Ananda*. So-Ham means *I AM That*. The sense of "I am" not "who I am." Yogis repeat this mantra silently over and over until thought dissolves, expanding their consciousness into cosmic consciousness. In terms of quantum physics, they transcend their individuality to pure being, which is the quantum field. So-Ham is a mantra used as a reminder that underneath your human experience, you are pure consciousness. The other mantra is Sat Chit Ananda. *Sat* means *truth*, *Chit* means *consciousness*, and *Ananda* means *bliss*. Truth. Consciousness. Bliss. The quality of pure consciousness is bliss. In other words, the nature of God is inexplicable joy. Beyond the mind is Sat Chit Ananda.

Let's connect the dots. So-Ham reminds you that you are pure consciousness. Sat Chit Ananda tells you that pure consciousness is bliss. This means the very nature of your being is total joy, total bliss, total ecstasy. Not because you accomplish something, just because you are here as a manifestation of the universe itself. As Rumi said, "You are not a drop in the ocean. You are the entire ocean in a drop." When you experience disharmony or any anxiety, you are only forgetting who you truly are. Meditation is a tool to quiet the mind so you can experience the entire ocean in a single drop. The purpose of life is to express itself as its true identity. To put it simply, you are here to understand and experience yourself as an individuation of divinity.

The universe is a contextual field. Existence is the dance between the unmanifested and the physical world—the realm of the absolute and the realm of the relative. Absolute is *being*, and relative is *experiencing*. The realm of the absolute never changes. This is the witness part inside yourself, the sense of I am. Absolute existence is absolute bliss (Sat Chit Ananda). The realm of the absolute is the plane of pure consciousness. On this plane, you cannot have any experience because you are all there is. In the absence of what you are not, it is impossible to experience who you are. The physical world is the same energy manifested in different patterns. This is the realm of the relative. Remember, every experience needs relativity. The universe is dualistic for you to experience it. To be right, you need someone to be wrong. For you to experience pleasure, pain has to exist. This dualistic world is created for divinity (pure consciousness) to know and experience itself through you.

God manifests itself in the realm of the relative through different patterns. Like a human plays basketball, tennis, or soccer, divinity plays the dog game, the tree game, the human game, and so on. The point of playing any game is to enjoy it. The reason the universe exists is to celebrate itself. Every New Years' Eve, people from all over the world light fireworks to celebrate another year has passed. Similarly, if you look at the sky, you can see all those stars as a firework show. Our universe is a celebration! Knowing this, I painted a large frame in which I wrote:

Every day is a celebration.
Every day is a celebration.
Every day is a celebration.

I put this frame in front of my bed with huge letters. Every time I wake up, the first thing I see is the reminder that today is a celebration. When you live every day celebrating existence, you start noticing the beauty in everything. This plane is gorgeous.

When I was younger, I used to throw big parties on my birthday. This past year, all my friends called me to celebrate it, but the desire to plan a party was not there because I have been celebrating existence every day for a while. I live joyfully and love how I spend my time. So, I spent my birthday writing this book, doing handstands, and enjoying whatever the day presented. If today were the last day of my life, I would do exactly what I am doing now. Every day is a celebration. It does not have to be your birthday to celebrate existence. Life is not meant to be an experience of fear and anxiety. It is intended to celebrate and experience who you really are: Ananda. Live every day as the witness of all creation, in pure joy. You are the gift of existence.

When you forget the dualistic nature of everything, funny things start to happen. You try to avoid pain and pursue pleasure. You act righteous and afraid that the other side of the coin may win. You need to understand that whatever is explicitly two is implicitly one. When someone is acting like a jackass instead of judging, be thankful for their existence. Thanks to this individual, you can experience yourself as their opposite. This is why Jesus said, "Love your enemies and pray for those who persecute you" He said this for two reasons. First, because implicitly, we are all one. Second, because explicitly, they are allowing you to experience the other side of the coin. You suffer because your righteousness is always tied to its opposite. Now another question arises: If we are all one, why are we separate? This is part of your nature. You are separate and one at the same time. The part of you that is one is the creator. The part that is separate is the creation. Can you allow for both?

Now, let's analyze two sides of the same coin: worry and laughter. Worry and laughter are the same feelings experienced from a different perspective. Have you seen someone who is so nervous they begin to laugh? Pain and pleasure are also the same. This is why many people feel pleasure through pain. Everything you experience is a vibration passing through your nervous system. The question is how are you going to interpret life? Is it going to be suffering, suffering, suffering? Or is it going to be laugh, laugh, laugh? Remember the dilemma of the zebra? The way you see it is entirely up to you.

A Buddha is a person who has awakened from the illusion of separateness. *Bu* comes from the Sanskrit word *Buddhi,* which means intellect, and *Dha* means one who is above. A Buddha is above duality. All Buddhas in history laughed when they got enlightened about the whole cosmic joke of existence. As Alan Watts quoted a Zen master, "When you attain satori, nothing is left for you at that moment but to have a good laugh." Or when Lin Chi was asked about enlightenment, he answered, "What can one do? I laughed and asked for a cup of tea." The moment you realize worry and laughter are implicitly one is when you transform anxiety into laughter.

A reporter once asked J. Krishnamurti, "What is your secret?" He answered, "Here is my secret: I don't mind what happens."

Krishnamurti lived in the plane of the absolute. Whatever happens here, in the realm of the relative, is always tied to its opposite and is constantly changing. So why bother worrying? Being okay with not knowing what is going to happen next means freedom. That's why he does not mind what happens.

Realize you see nothing but yourself expressed differently. When you catch yourself judging another person like a drunk or a liar, say, "There I go again, being a drunk" or "There I go again, being an exquisite liar." Once you remember who you are and why you are here, you can begin celebrating every day of your existence.

Love is the purpose of duality. Love is the fabric of the universe. Just like the nature of a flower is to smell good, the nature of your being is Ananda. The fabric of life is pure joy. Enjoy the opportunity existence has given you. Celebrate it as much as possible. Stop wasting time trying to be right. Do not get trapped in duality.

Let's change this world by the method of celebration— by singing, by dancing, by loving, by sharing, by creating, by meditating, by laughing. Not by fighting. Not by worrying. Not by righteousness. In the realm of the relative, you are here to express and experience the broadest version you have ever dared to think about yourself. Life is a glorious experience. And remember, if you want to know God, which is ultimately yourself, learn how to be joyful.

THE ULTIMATE MATRIX

THE MOVIE *THE MATRIX* MIRRORS HOW A PERSON LIVES IN THE prison of their subconscious mind. Neo (Keanu Reeves) is a computer hacker who is searching for deeper meaning in his life. He meets a mysterious being, Morpheus (Laurence Fishburne), who gives him a choice: either to take a blue pill or a red pill. If he takes the blue pill, he will wake up tomorrow as if nothing happened, but if he takes the red pill, he will uncover the truth and see reality for what it truly is. He decides to take the red pill and finds that what he calls reality is really a computer program called the matrix.

Morpheus says, "What is real? How do you define *real*? If you're talking about what you can feel, what you can smell, what you can taste, and see, then *real* is simply electrical signals interpreted by your brain." Morpheus is helping Neo liberate himself and explains that every human inside the matrix is born as a slave, "born into a prison that you cannot smell or taste or touch. A prison for your mind." Sound familiar?

Every person on the planet is conditioned. Your conditioning makes you perceive reality through a limited perspective. Your programming was written in your subconscious and dictates how you behave 95 percent of the day. When you live according to a program, you live in a mental prison.

My work is about transforming unconsciousness into consciousness. I wrote this book to help you realize what is making you suffer is your identification with the mind and your subconscious programming. The moment you change your internal narrative is the moment you adjust your relationship to life. When you create space from your mental patterns, you discover you are more than what you are concerned about. The only thing that is making you suffer is your mind and the lack of understanding it.

When you understand the root of your behavior and the power of your being, you rapidly find freedom. My main product is freedom. However, if I were to go to the park and tell someone that I am going to help them free themselves, they would look at me as if I am insane. If you do not know you are in prison, what do you do? You upgrade your cell by trying to have a bigger TV. You cannot escape if you do not know you are in prison in the first place. You perceive the world based on your conditioning, reacting predictably. You pursue goal after goal, sailing without a compass. You defend whatever your environment taught you, trying to be right and making others wrong. You live scared, protecting yourself from imaginary worries. The people inside the matrix do not know they are living according to a program— do you?

Your desire system creates your perceptual universe. Who you think you are is a matter of perspective. How many people define themselves by their professions? Like Bob, the guy who sells furniture. Or Linda, the daughter of the singer who is now a waiter. Defining yourself as your profession limits you because you forget who you truly are. Whatever you define yourself as you will protect because it gives you a sense of identity. You are afraid of losing what is making you a slave in the first place. Strange paradox. Whatever you do, do not limit your magnificence by believing you are *only* that.

The concept of yourself is conditioned, like the minds of the people living in the matrix. Desire affects perception. You only notice whatever you believe you are lacking. If you feel insecure about your nose, you are only going to notice other people's noses. The moment you see a person who has what you want, your mind will make you believe they have it because of their pretty nose. Do you think the universe ran out of noses to give? What is a pretty nose anyway? Is this not a mental prison? Everything you notice is a reflection of your attachments.

If you see yourself as unworthy, you subconsciously overcompensate in every other area of your life to protect this limited belief. No matter what you accomplish, if you do not know the root of your behavior, the feeling of unworthiness will still dictate your actions.

The mind loves to trick you with the "if only" story. "If only I was younger ..." "If only I was older ..." "If only I lost ten pounds ..." "If only I get the promotion ..." "If only I meet a partner ..." The illusion is that if you get just a little bit more, it will be enough. This moment is already absolutely perfect. When an "if only" happens, you are living in the matrix. Take the red pill and appreciate the present moment. Free yourself from these wrong identifications. Liberate yourself from your conditioning.

To live in the known is bondage. To live in the unknown is liberation.

Yogis describe the world as *Maya*. In Sanskrit, Maya means illusion. Similarly, the Toltecs describe the world as *Mitote*, which means something you believe is real is actually not. The illusion comes when you believe you are your thoughts instead of the awareness behind them watching how everything unfolds. What you perceive is relative reality or Maya.

Alan Watts describes this scenario:

> Let's suppose that you were able every night to dream any dream that you wanted to dream. And that you could, for example, have the power within one night to dream seventy-five years of time. Or any length of time you wanted to have. And you would, naturally as you began on this adventure of dreams, you would fulfill all your wishes. You would have every kind of pleasure you could conceive. And after several nights of seventy-five years of total pleasure each, you would say "Well, that was pretty great." But now let's have a surprise. Let's have a dream which isn't under control. Where something is gonna happen to me that I don't know what it's going to be. And you would dig that and come out of that and say "Wow, that was a close shave, wasn't it?" And then you would get more and more adventurous, and you would make further and further out gambles as to what you would dream. And finally, you

would dream … where you are now! You would dream the dream of living the life that you are actually living today. That would be within the infinite multiplicity of the choices you would have. Of playing that you weren't God. Because the whole nature of the godhead, according to this idea, is to play that he's not.

Seeing the universe as drama (Lila) is forgetting that you are dreaming. God is playing hide-and-seek because it is the only way it can find itself. Remember, God is described in terms of quantum physics and every scripture as omnipresent. Nothing can exist apart or separate from it. This includes you. Yet, you forgot who you really are to experience the surprise that is your life. You forget that you are God in disguise to find yourself. You forgot you are dreaming. The realm of the relative is Maya because everything is constantly changing. Maya is making you believe that the dream is real. Remembering who you really are is waking up from the dream. This is why enlightenment is called awakening.

What happens outside yourself is inseparable from what happens inside. Every out has an in, and every in has an out. They are one, just like you and everything else. What is limiting you from experiencing the whole universe as yourself is just a psychological boundary. The illusion of separation disappears when you start creating space between you and your thoughts. The moment you transcend thought, you begin to wake up and experience reality as it truly is. Enlightened beings see the world as Maya (or people who do psychedelics). Duality becomes unity.

What experience makes you feel one with all? Easy, when you are in love! Being love is taking the red pill. Love makes everything taste better, every song more beautiful, and every sunset more magical. You act mindful, conscious, and selfless. Being in a state of love does not allow worry to come in. Love makes you present; it makes you live outside the matrix. When you are free from your self-imposed prison, you are in love with the entire world because you realize that the whole universe is inside you. Love is unity. Fear is the illusion of separation.

How do you wake up someone from inside a dream? In *The Matrix*, Morpheus is playing the role of a guru. A guru literally means a remover of darkness. It is not necessarily someone physical because it already exists inside yourself. If you pay attention, the entire universe is your guru. The purpose of a guru is to liberate you from Maya. As Ram Dass says, "A guru is not just a groovy teacher—it is your doorway to the beyond."

Like Morpheus helped Neo get liberated from the matrix, your guru appears in the form of intuition. Intuition is the way your inner self and the universe communicate with you. As an enlightened being, Ramana Maharshi said, "God, guru, and self are the same."

In India, there is a term for awakening called *Dwijas*. Dwijas in Sanskrit means "twice born." The first birth is from your mother's womb. The second is when you wake up out of your own awareness. Jesus' resurrection refers to this—not the body coming back from the dead but the birth of Christ's consciousness or enlightenment. When you quiet the mind, you access your full intelligence and receive intuitive signals. When you begin playing with these signals, opportunities start opening in your life. The whole universe is trying to express itself through you. Let it! Be an open channel. Anything you do, do it from a place of love, and you automatically are going to fulfill your duty on this planet.

Basically, this is how it is: Human discontentment is just a simple case of mistaken identity. Once you become aware of your divinity, you automatically see it in others. Then it is only natural to regard yourself and everyone else as God. When you experience truth, morality is no longer needed. You are looking for God everywhere but here. That is why you cannot find it. God can only be found in the present moment. Not in worrying about the past or overthinking the future. It is all now.

There is a part of *The Matrix* when Cypher (Joe Pantoliano) regrets taking the red pill. He incessantly complains about the tasteless food, his tiny bed, and living on a spaceship in constant battle. This is when the movie and real life are so different. No enlightened being has ever wanted to go back to being a prisoner of their mind. Without awareness, you have no choice because you live in reaction to your subconscious programming and conditioning. Awareness makes you recover your free will. You have everything you need to experience bliss … right now!

When you realize you lack nothing, everything becomes available. When you awaken, you step out of the ultimate matrix and realize the miracle of this moment. Food tastes better, the walk in the park is more amusing, the work you do is more fulfilling, and the conversations you have are more intimate. No matter what happens around you, your state of gratitude and appreciation for life is always there. Taking the red pill is realizing that you are the awareness looking at the miracle of life. Taking the red pill means you are always acting from a place of love. Taking the red pill is understanding who you truly are, Sat Chit Ananda, or infinite bliss. And don't forget ... this is a dream. Enjoy it!

LOVE HURTS ... NO, IT DOESN'T

EVERYONE ALWAYS TELLS US TO BE LOVING, TO LOVE EVERYONE, and to love ourselves. But have you ever questioned what love actually is? Love cannot be explained with words. That is why if you read a love poem, you would not be able to experience it. Because love is not something you *do*; it is something you *are*.

So, what is love after all? Is love pleasure? Is love desire? Is love sex? Is love possession? Is love control? Can there be love if you want something in return? The best way to start understanding love is by analyzing what it is not. Love is not possession. You tend to put conditions on love because you learn it from a young age. Your parents, even though they love you, placed conditions on you. As a kid, you believed if you did not behave as your parents told you to, they would not love you anymore. You learned that love can be taken away and that it is something you earn and not something you are. To this day, I have many friends who believe that if they do not marry a certain partner, of whom their parents approve, their parents will not love them anymore.

Conditional love is when you say I love you as long as you ... "behave the way I want you to," "only have sex with me," "believe in the same God as me," or "do whatever I tell you." If you place any conditions on love, understand that this has nothing to do with love; this is only about yourself. Conditional love is the opposite of what love actually is. Love is not controlling. Love is not manipulating. It is not possessing. Love has no conditions. It cannot be demanded. Where there is love, there are no expectations, demands, or dependencies. Love is not a destination. It is not a product. It does not need anyone or anything to appear. It is the expression of your being. Love is all-embracing. The entire business of love starts and ends with yourself because you are it.

As a human, you only have two choices: you can either act from a place of fear or a place of love. Often, what you call love is the desire to control and possess. Control is a mask of insecurity, which is fear. Fear is the misconception that someone else can give you something you already have. When you fall in love with someone, that person is not giving you love. They are only allowing you to touch the place within you to experience the love you already are. The person is simply the vehicle that reveals your true essence. The illusion comes when you think they are the source of the love you experience. When you forget that, funny things start to happen. You begin to worry you will lose your supply or that you are going to run out of love. This is when you shift from love to fear.

A fear-based love experience is jealousy. You believe you are acting jealous because you love your partner so much, but you are acting with a defense mechanism of losing your supply. Relationships are a great tool to reveal where you need to grow.

Your sense of inadequacy is already in you, but the way you experience it is through a sense of jealousy and control.

Out of fear, more fear is born. Out of love, more love is born. Fear feels like control, and love feels like letting go. When you make decisions out of fear, you close and contract; when you make them out of love, you expand. Love has no obligations, but fear has many. Love has no expectations, and fear has many. The byproduct of fear is suffering, and the byproduct of love is joy. To act from fear is bondage. To act from love is freedom. What has to happen for you to feel worthy of experiencing yourself as you really are? Stop polishing your ignorance. Stop trying to defend your fears because dependency is misery.

People aspire to find their other half and believe once they find it, they will finally be complete. This is insane! It implies you are not already complete. Let me finish these cliché phrases for you: You complete me ... no, you don't! Love is blind ... no, it's not! Ignorance is bliss ... no, it's not! Love hurts ... no, it doesn't!

Relationships are meant for sharing your joy—not about taking it from others. A powerful relationship is when the people involved understand they are two wholes sharing their experience. They both know the source of love is never going to run out. A mind that is afraid has no capacity to love. It always acts defensively and expects something in return.

Let's start analyzing these clichés: Love is blind ... no, it's not! Fear is blind. Attachments and control are blind. Love sees everything as a part of themselves; it can never be blind. Love hurts ... no, it doesn't! Fear hurts. Love doesn't. You may believe that love can be painful if you see someone else as your other half. You act possessive and call it love. True love has nothing to do with this because true love does not want anything whatsoever. The only type of love that can hurt is conditional love. And conditional love is only about you.

Why do people say they want to fall in love? Because they need someone else to pick them up. Instead of falling in love, rise in love. Rising in love is not a relationship. It is a state of being. Falling in love is with one person. Rising in love is with the whole universe. When you rise in love, you become it, and whatever happens, you give it unconditionally. Falling in love looks like bondage, and rising in love looks like freedom.

The most remarkable characteristic of rising in love is that it is unlimited. Like, if you have one dollar and give half of it away, you only have fifty cents. However, if you give all of your love away, you still have all of your love left! You cannot *collect* love. You can only *be* it. Love does not bargain; it only gives and gives and gives. Love cannot be measured because it is infinite.

Love is recognizing yourself in the person in front of you. It is a sense of oneness. Love never hurts. It does not demand that you do anything. Love is not a responsibility. It is not a duty. Love is your joy. Do whatever you do out of joy and not a sense of responsibility. Obligations cannot exist in real love.

Love is equal to:

- you
- God
- truth
- consciousness
- all there is
- the fabric of life

Ignorance is believing the source of love is external. The root of pain is to be ignorant of yourself. They say that ignorance is bliss ... no, it's not! If ignorance was bliss, why are there not more happy people? I am not talking about intellectual knowledge; I am referring to the ignorance of not knowing who you truly are, loving awareness. To know yourself is bliss; to forget is sorrow. Greed, anger, and bitterness are ignorance. Not knowing you are the source of love is ignorance.

When you forget you are the source, you start searching for love in other people. Only when you truly understand you need nothing from others can you start experiencing yourself as the source. The purpose of relationships is to share your completeness and not to experience your incompleteness. Love is not a relationship; it is who you are. The more you source it, the more you experience it. And the more love you experience, the fewer demands you make. When you search for love in others, you tend to put conditions on it: "I love you if ..." In love, there are no *ifs*. You might even say, "I think I love you," but love has nothing to do with thinking! Love is not a technique; it is understanding. Love is not an experience; it is who you are. Make every moment of your life a loving moment. These are signs that appear when you are getting to know your true self:

- a sense of ease
- freedom from stress and anxiety
- freedom from control and possessiveness
- living in joy and harmony
- abundant energy available at all times

Charles Darwin said that the fundamental instinct of a human being was survival. Survival is not your fundamental instinct; *love* is. If you see a child walking in the middle of the street and a car is approaching, your instinct is to run and save the kid—not to run away. You do not make calculations if you are going to get hurt or even be able to save the child. You are acting by instinct. So please remember, love is your *fundamental instinct*.

The greatest gift you can learn in life is what love is really about. It has nothing to do with the outside. You do not need anyone or anything to give it to you. You have an unlimited supply inside you. So, do not be tacky! Give it to everyone! Can a flower only give its fragrance to the people it likes? Obviously not! So, why are you only giving love to a finite amount of people? If you are in a relationship, thank them because your partner allows you to experience what love truly is. If you had an abusive relationship, also thank them because they taught you what conditional love looks like. Remember, it is in the condition that you are not that allows you to experience what you are.

When you are in love with someone, you want to merge and be one with that person. Making yourself into one with the whole universe has a better name: Yoga. Why are you limiting yourself to only one person? I am not saying to have orgies and be in romantic relationships with everybody. I am simply saying that when you polish your own mirror and reflect the love you are, you will rise in love with existence. Love always comes with awareness. Love is awareness in action. Awareness never fights; it always releases. Awareness is knowledge, and knowledge is bliss.

Love is more than an idea. It is a state of being. When you

are in love, you enjoy everything you do. Realize there is no separation between you and love. You are it. Next time you get hurt, remember that it is fear that makes you hurt, not love, because love hurts ... no, it doesn't!

OBVIOUSLY, LIFE IS SETTING ME UP FOR SUCCESS

WHERE DO YOU WAKE UP EVERY DAY? WHAT IS THIS PLACE anyway? It turns out it is the realm of the relative. Relativity is the only way you can have any type of experience. If everybody in the world were as good as Lebron James is at playing basketball, nobody could experience being the best in the world.

All opposites are equals. That is the paradox of this dimension. All experiences in life are double binds because any direction you take implies moving away from its opposite. The biggest paradox is the one of *being and becoming*. Clearly, you are growing and evolving—but only to reveal who you already are. Strange paradox. The universe is relative because it is the only way the universe can experience itself. You are not a person experiencing the universe; you are the universe experiencing itself through a person. Through you, the universe is becoming more aware of itself.

Obviously, the entire cosmos exists for this moment. It is the only way the game can be designed. It is like when you find a twenty-dollar bill in an old jacket. You have way more money in your bank account, but those twenty bucks, for some reason, tastes different. Forgetting that you put the money in your pocket was essential for the surprise. Similarly, you put yourself in the situation you are in right now and forgot about it to experience the wonder of realizing who you really are. This is the paradox of attaining enlightenment because trying to become a Buddha is negating the fact you already are one. The only difference between you and a Buddha is that he remembers and you do not. Life does not move from imperfection to perfection; it always moves from perfection to perfection. Existence is perfect because it lacks nothing. Perfection is not an achievement. That's why enlightenment is not a goal. It is only a realization.

So, how can you attain enlightenment? You have to do it without intending to. The more you try, the more you miss. Security can only be obtained when you embrace insecurity. Strange paradox. You have to find a way to live spontaneously, which is an impossible task. It is like saying, "I'm going to plan how to scare myself," but to actually get scared, you have to be surprised. You cannot plan it because the second you know what will happen, it ceases to be scary. You cannot surprise yourself on purpose, but that is what you have to do. Strange paradox.

Everything happens according to cosmic law. Cosmic laws are the rules of nature that create, maintain, and dissolve the universe. Existence happens spontaneously, within your experience, and in the entire cosmos. Love, death, and life arise spontaneously. Once you observe your behavior, you realize you cannot help but be spontaneous. You do not make preparations to breathe or for your heart to keep beating. Your dog does not plan to get excited when he sees you, and if you see someone you love, you cannot help but smile. You do not plan on it; it just happens.

In Taoism, nature and spontaneity are the same words, *Tzu*

Jan. Tzu Jan means that existence happens spontaneously, not according to plan. You cannot make yourself fall in love with someone, but you cannot help it either. Enlightenment works the same way; it has to happen on its own. Because the self you are trying to improve does not exist. You cannot speed it up, and you cannot slow it down. Your pace is absolutely perfect. When you are ready to wake up, you will. Everything you want to achieve is already inside you.

The trap of ignorance is the only trap there is; the mind is making you believe you are a separate self. Your conditioning makes you react predictably, which blocks the spontaneity of your true nature. Your thoughts are recycling from the past, which blocks you from acting spontaneously. This is the difference between acting and reacting. Action is spontaneous, and reaction always happens according to your conditioning. Action is creative, and reaction is predictable.

If you think your way through existence, you are always missing it. This is why Zen teaches the art of archery by aiming and shooting simultaneously. Because the moment they begin to think, they are already too late. The arrow and archer need to become one, so there is no delay. This also happens in sports. I was watching an NFL game, and a defensive player made an unbelievable play. Somehow, instinctively, he knew where the opposing quarterback was going to throw the ball. He did not have the time to think about it because he would be a second too late and miss the chance of making an interception. Similarly, if you are always thinking, you are always a little too late.

Why are you so afraid of living spontaneously? Being makes you act spontaneously, but thinking makes you react predictably.

Being makes you experience unity, but thinking makes you experience separateness. Knowledge is always in duality, but understanding transcends it. Understanding is another dimension. As a flower naturally blooms, the life within you is trying to find joyful expression. Let it! You are the best in the world at something. Cultivate your inner genius by quieting your mind so you can give it to the rest of existence. Anxiety is only born out of imagination. Success, joy, and bliss happen spontaneously. To always be learning, discovering, and unfolding is your dharma. Beyond the mind is the direct experience of being, knowing, and loving.

The game in the realm of the relative is to experience and know yourself through situations, relationships, work, friendship, family, and anything you can imagine. When you cultivate higher levels of awareness, you understand that conflict under one perspective means harmony in a higher one. The gut is known as the second brain of the body, but if you see its cells under a microscope, different types of bacteria are always fighting each other. Yet, if you zoom out, the constant battle of bacteria is what is keeping you alive.

From a higher perspective, situations are always harmonious. Neem Karoli Baba, an enlightened being, when asked about war, answered, "Don't you see it's all perfect?" The higher you go, the fewer distinctions exist. From an airplane, you cannot perceive the difference between Mexico and America. If you go higher and see the earth from a spaceship, the earth appears as one. Where is India? Or Brazil? Where are the capitalists or the socialists? From a higher perspective, duality becomes unity.

Suffering is part of the perfection of the universe. If you zoom out, suffering is grace. Sometimes you do not understand suffering because you are looking at it through a microscope. When time passes, you realize that you cannot be the evolved being you are now without it. Stop your nonsense about holding grudges and being resentful about something that happened in the past. If you are going to blame someone, blame them entirely. Yes, they created some suffering, but they also stimulated the magnificent being you are right now. It is impossible to isolate a single fact or event that has ever happened. Like when did you get born? Was it when you took your first breath? Or when your parents conceived you? Or when your parents met? Or when your grandparents met?

Interpreting single events makes as much sense as translating a Russian novel into Sanskrit while only speaking English. In other words, it is a complete and absurd waste of time. All that happens is the cause of all that happens. The idea of a single incident is an illusion. Life is not looking for an explanation. It is looking for you to experience it.

Mooji says, "The world is not what you think it is. The world is exactly what you think it is. Find the place within you where both these statements are true." Knowing you are God in disguise, playing hide-and-seek with yourself, you are never given an obstacle you cannot overcome because you set your own trap. Knowing there is no separation between you and the quantum field. Knowing the paradox of being and becoming, knowing that you already are a Buddha but forgot, and that enlightenment happens by itself. The only rational explanation of the metaphysics of the universe is this: Of course, life is setting you up for success.

Life is setting you up for success because you set up your own trap. You set your own trap and forgot about it, so you can spontaneously get out of it. You know all the answers for the test are within you, but you forgot about them, so you can experience getting an A or maybe an F. You know the way out of the maze, but you forgot and got lost on purpose for the game to be fun. You are here to taste the chocolate.

As Maharishi Mahesh Yogi said, "Expansion of happiness is the purpose of creation." You are here to express and experience the highest version you ever dare think about yourself. In reality, you are the student, the teacher, and the dean all at the same time. Because ultimately, the essence of each and every one of us is one. To be alive, to be here now, fully enjoying this moment is the most you can do. Life is beyond any meaning you can find. Life needs no meaning because life is already complete. Relax, do not get worried. Everything is ready for celebration; nothing is missing.

It is like the Zen story when a student asked, "What is the best method to attain liberation or enlightenment?"

The master answered, "Who binds you?"

No one is binding you. In the absence of all judgment comes freedom. You are the source of your own experience. Sometimes you forget who you are, and that's amazing. That is part of the game. Everything in this book is only a reminder of what you already know. All the answers are inside you. All the bliss is inside you. All the universe is inside you. The most incredible things in life, you did not plan, you did not expect, they just happened. Life simply unfolded.

If you remember who you are, I dare you to make the same claim that I did (because no one is going to declare it for you): I choose myself as an example for humanity. By living my life,

I will remind others who they really are. Watch me! Watch how I respond to whatever life throws at me. If I act knowing everything is a part of myself, I can heal the world. The more I work on myself, the more I can reflect the love that I am back to others. The only reason I am here is to give you back to yourself.

Go out into the world. It is a beautiful, adventurous challenge. Do not miss the opportunity to explore it. And go out without fear. There is nothing to be scared of. Just remember to constantly quiet your mind and experience the silence and wisdom within. Live life 200 percent! Never forget this: Every day is a celebration … because obviously life is setting me up for success.

REFERENCES

Ford, Henry. "Whether you believe you can do a thing or not, you are right." Quote Investigator. https://quoteinvestigator.com/2015/02/03/you-can/.

Aurelius, M., & Waterfield, R. (2021). *Meditations: The Annotated Edition* (Annotated ed.). Basic Books.

Lakhiani, Vishen. *Summary of the Code of Extraordinary Minds: 10 Unconventional Laws to Redefine Your Life and Succeed On Your Own Terms: Conversation Starters.* Independently published.

Benjamin Franklin FAQ. (October 22, 2019). The Franklin Institute. https://www.fi.edu/benjamin-franklin-faq.

Braden, G. (2021). *The Divine Matrix: Bridging Time, Space, Miracles, and Belief by Gregg Braden(2008–01-02).* Hay House.

Bressan, D. (2020, January 7). *Nikola Tesla's Earthquake Machine.* Forbes. https://www.forbes.com/sites/davidbressan/2020/01/07/nikola-teslas-earthquake-machine/?sh=4671ba2452c5

Burt, J. C. (2021). *Nietzsche and God is Dead.* Blurb.

Carrey, J., & Vachon, D. (2021). *Memoirs and Misinformation: A novel.* Vintage.

Carse, J. (2013). *Finite and Infinite Games.* Free Press.

Chopra, D. (2008). *Buddha: A Story of Enlightenment (Enlightenment Series, 1).* HarperOne.

Chopra, D. (2009). *The Seven Spiritual Laws of Success: A Practical Guide to the Fulfillment of Your Dreams (16pt Large Print Edition).* ReadHowYouWant.

Csikszentmihalyi, M. (2008). *Flow: The Psychology of Optimal Experience (Harper Perennial Modern Classics)* (1st ed.). Harper Perennial Modern Classics.

Dass, R. (1978). *Be Here Now.* Harmony.

Dass, R., Das, R., & True, S. (2014). *Polishing the Mirror.* Sounds True.

DeMello, A. (2021a). *Awareness: The Perils and Opportunities of Reality by Anthony De Mello (1990) Paperback.* Image Books.

DeMello, A. (2021b). *Awareness: The Perils and Opportunities of Reality by Anthony De Mello (1990) Paperback.* Image Books.

Descartes, R. (2021). *Discourse on the Method-Classic Edition(Annotated).* Independently published.

Disney, W. (2016, June 6). *Worry is a misuse of imagination.* Philosiblog. https://philosiblog.com/2016/06/06/worry-is-a-misuse-of-imagination/

Dispenza, J. D. (2019). *Becoming Supernatural: How Common People Are Doing the Uncommon* (Illustrated ed.). Hay House Inc.

"Don't do STUPID Things!" - Jordan B. Peterson (@jordanbpeterson) - #Entspresso. (2017, September 26). [Video]. YouTube. https://www.youtube.com/watch?v=Z1OsY8_I8eg.

Dyer, D. W. W. (2021). *Power of Awakening, The: Mindfulness Practices and Spiritual Tools to Transform Your Life.* Hay House Inc.

Frankl, V. E. (2021). *Man's Search for Meaning 1st (first) edition Text Only.* Penguin Random House.

Full Speech: Jim Carrey's Commencement Address at the 2014 MUM Graduation (EN, FR, ES, RU, GR, …). (2014, May 30). [Video]. YouTube. https://www.youtube.com/watch?v=V80-gPkpH6M.

Goddard, N., & Collection, T. N. (2020). *The Neville Collection: All 10 Books by a Modern Master.* Independently published.

Greene, R. (2021). *The 48 Laws of Power.* Viva Books PRIVATE LIMITED.

Hawking, S. (2018). *Brief Answers to the Big Questions.* JOHN MURRAY.

Hicks, E., & Hicks, J. (2015). *The Essential Law of Attraction Collection* (Reprint ed.). Hay House Inc.

Hill, N., & Horowitz, M. (2019). *Think and Grow Rich (Original Classic Edition)* (Original ed.). G&D Media.

How To Deal With the Uncertainty of Life? - Sadhguru. (2018, November 22). [Video]. YouTube. https://www.youtube.com/watch?v=Rx6LAB1-BHI.

Initiates, T. (2021). *The Kybalion: Hermetic Philosophy.* Independently published.

Jung, C. G. (2003). *Psychology of the Unconscious.* Dover Publications.

Kabat-Zinn, J. (2010). *Wherever You Go, There You Are: Mindfulness Meditation In Everyday Life* (1st ed.). Hachette Books.

The King Center | The Center for Nonviolent Social Change. (2021, June 26). The King Center. https://thekingcenter.org.

Kiyosaki, R. T. (2020). *Rich Dad Poor Dad: What the Rich Teach their Kids About Money That The Poor And Middle Class Do Not!* (Illustrated ed.). Bespoke Books.

Krishnamurti, J., & Lutyens, M. (2009). *Freedom from the Known* (Later Edition). HarperSanFrancisco.

Lipton, B. H. (2021). *By Bruce H. Lipton - The Biology of Belief: Unleashing the Power of Consciousness, Matter and Miracles (1st Edition) (2/13/05)* (8th Printing ed.). Mountain of Love Productions, Incorporated.

Lott, T. (2018, February 14). *Jordan Peterson: 'The pursuit of happiness is a pointless goal.'* The Guardian. https://www.theguardian.com/global/2018/jan/21/jordan-peterson-self-help-author-12-steps-interview.

Lynch, D. (2021). *Catching the Big Fish: Meditation, Consciousness and Creativity by David Lynch (2007-10-04).* Michael Joseph.

Lucas, G. (Director). *Star Wars IV: A New Hope.* (1977). Twentieth Century Fox.

M. (2017). *White Fire: Spiritual Insights and Teachings of Advaita Zen Master Mooji* (Illustrated ed.). Non-Duality.

Maharaj, S. N., Mehta, S., & Kshirsagar, D. (2014). *Meditations With Sri Nisargadatta Maharaj* (1st ed.). Yogi Impressions Books Pvt. Ltd.

"May Your Dreams NOT be Fulfilled" – Sadhguru's Blessing. (2019, June 17). [Video]. YouTube. https://www.youtube.com/watch?v=WPsuHTnPLE4

Michael Jordan's Basketball Hall of Fame Enshrinement Speech. (2012, February 21). [Video]. YouTube. https://www.youtube.com/watch?v=XLzBMGXfK4c.

M.M.Y. (2019). *Science of Being and Art of Living.* Diana.

Mondi, D. W., & Crowley, R. (2015). *BUDDHISM: A Beginner's Guide to Buddhism: Your Path to a Meaningful Life (Simplicity - Zen - Meditation - Calm - Buddhist Philosophy - Happiness - Yoga - Buddha).* Red Dragon Publishing.

Murphy, J. (2021). *The Power of Your Subconscious Mind.* Reprint.

Not Minding What Happens, Eckhart Tolle. (n.d.). Awakin.org. Retrieved June 29, 2021, from https://www.awakin.org/read/view.php?tid=2089

Osho, O. (1997). *Intimacy: Trusting Oneself and the Other* (First ed.). St. Martin's Griffin.

Ortega. K. (Director). (2009). *This is It* [Film]. Columbia Pictures.

P. (2021b). *The Last Days of Socrates (Penguin Classics) by Plato(2011–01-25)*. Penguin Classics.

Palahniuk, C. (2018). *Fight Club: A Novel* (Reissue ed.). W. W. Norton & Company.

The Physics of Spirituality | Nassim Haramein with Vishen Lakhiani. (2019, May 17). [Video]. YouTube. https://www.youtube.com/watch?v=gj5zRx7G_cs.

Ruiz, D. M. (2021). *Don Miguel Ruiz Toltec Wisdom Series Collection 3 Books Set,(The Four Agreements: Practical Guide to Personal Freedom, The Mastery of Love and The Fifth Agreement)*. Amber-Allen Publishing.

S. (2016). *Inner Engineering: A Yogi's Guide to Joy* (1ˢᵗ ed.). Harmony.

Satchidananda, S. (2012). *The Yoga Sutras of Patanjali: Commentary on the Raja Yoga Sutras by Sri Swami Satchidananda*. Integral Yoga Publications.

Seneca, L. A., & Gummere, R. (2021). *Letters from a Stoic: Seneca's Moral Letters to Lucilius*. Independently published.

Shakespeare, W. (2020). *Hamlet by William Shakespeare*. Independently published.

Simmons, M. W. (2016). *Thomas Edison: American Inventor*. CreateSpace Independent Publishing Platform.

Singer, M. A. (2015). *The Surrender Experiment: My Journey into Life's Perfection* (Illustrated ed.). Harmony.

Suzuki, D. T., & Jung, C. (1994). *An Introduction to Zen Buddhism* (Reissue ed.). Grove Press.

Suzuki, S. (2021). *Zen Mind, Beginner's Mind (Shambhala Library) 1ˢᵗ (first) edition Text Only* (1St Edition). Weatherhill Distribution Inc.

To Know Yourself: Essential Teachings of Swami Satchidananda by Sri Swami Satchidananda (1988–12-27). (2021). Integral Yoga Publications.

Tolle, E. (2008). *A New Earth: Awakening to Your Life's Purpose (Oprah's Book Club, Selection 61)* (Reprint ed.). Penguin.

Tshering, A. (2019, May 7). *Alan Watt's Backwards Law And 3 Ways It Can Help With Your Mental Health*. Anthony Tshering, LCSW. http://www.brooklyntherapist.net/blog/2018/6/12/alan-watts-backwards-law.

Tyson, N., & Trefil, J. (2021). *Cosmic Queries: StarTalk's Guide to Who We Are, How We Got Here, and Where We're Going*. National Geographic.

Walsch, N. D. (1996). *Conversations with God: An Uncommon Dialogue, Book 1 (Conversations with God Series)* (1ˢᵗ ed.). TarcherPerigee.

Walsch, N. D. (2021). *The Complete Conversations with God* (Reprint ed.). Perigee Books US.

Watts, A. (2021, March 21). *Quotes*. Alan Watts Organization. https://alanwatts.org/quotes/

The Way of Zen by Watts, Alan W.(January 26, 1999) Paperback. (2021). Vintage.

Wolinsky, S. (2020). *I Am That I Am: A Tribute to Sri Nisargadatta Maharaj*. Self.